EMOTIONAL

Vampires

EMOTIONAL
VAMPIRES

How to Protect Your Happiness
From People Who Suck Yours Dry

COACH DANIEL RATNER

Copyright Notice

© 2025 Coach Ratner. All rights reserved.

No part of this book may be reproduced, distributed,
or transmitted in any form or by any means,
including photocopying, recording,
or other electronic or mechanical methods, without
the prior written permission of the publisher, except
in the case of brief quotations embodied in critical
reviews and certain other noncommercial
uses permitted by copyright law.

Book cover & interior design by:
Joanna & Grzegorz Japoł - LUNA Design Studio

Table of Contents

Start Here	7
Categories of Emotional Vampires	11
The Perpetual Victim	14
The Narcissist	25
The Drama Queen	46
The Socially Awkward	52
Emotional Constipation	62
Parents, Brothers, Sisters, Spouses, or In-laws	70
Boundary Invaders	75
The Second Guessers	80
The Projectors	84
The Overly Dependent	94
Non-Stop Talkers	101
Teenagers: Where Logic Doesn't Exist	106
The Terrible Twos	111
Are You an Emotional Vampire?	116
The Friendship Audit	124
What True Friendship Really Is	130
How to Make Relationships Healthy	137
Not All Apologies Are the Same	159
3 Levels of Forgiveness	167
Find Your Keepers	172
About the Author	191
Preview of When Botox Meets Bezos	192

Start Here

She was a 10 out of 10 by most people who met her. Charming, charismatic, and effortlessly engaging were her best attributes—the kind of person who lit up a room just by walking into it. How could it be that such a stunning, captivating woman remained unmarried?

Most Friday nights, she joined our family for dinner, and we genuinely enjoyed her presence. But over time, a subtle truth began to reveal itself—not all at once, but slowly, like the final drips of a pour-over coffee from freshly ground beans. At first, it was warm and welcome, but eventually, those drips began to feel more like murky water seeping from a rusted, long-abandoned water heater.

When that starts to happen, what once felt like a gift, ends up becoming a burden. She was draining my entire family of emotional energy. This is when the term "Emotional Vampires," started to make headway in our family's vernacular.

Never in a million years did we suspect that beneath her charm lurked something far more insidious. At best, she was intensely self-absorbed; at worst, a full-blown narcissist. But she wasn't a social media influencer chasing likes or a politician craving the spotlight—typical arenas for those who thrive on attention. Instead, she made our home her stage, quietly becoming the center of our lives.

It's like being in an unhealthy relationship—you don't recognize just how toxic it is until after the breakup. Only then do you feel the immense relief, as if a massive weight has been lifted off your back. That's when you realize how much the heavy burden has been weighing you down.

The same is true for Emotional Vampires. They sap your energy, but it's often only when they're no longer in your life that you fully grasp how unhealthy the dynamic was.

We all encounter Emotional Vampires in our lives. Some are unavoidable, like certain family members; some may be our friends, while others enter our lives due to circumstances. The purpose of this book is to empower you to protect your happiness. You are in control of who you allow into your life and who you need to stay away from. Knowing which ones drain you of your emotional energy will allow you to be more in control of your emotional well-being. For the people that have to be in your life, learning how to establish boundaries will help you to manage these difficult relationships. By becoming more intentional and strategic with who you spend your time with, you can safeguard your happiness.

We will begin by categorizing Emotional Vampires into various groups, acknowledging that someone can belong to multiple categories. Once we identify the category or categories they fall into, the next step is to assess their role in our lives. If there is no meaningful reason for their presence, we should consider whether we might be better off without them. However, if their presence is essential, like your parents, siblings, clients, or even a large donor, we must explore ways to make the relationship healthier. Ultimately, the goal of this book is to help us identify and cherish the "Keepers" in our lives—those who bring ease, positivity, and a sense of peace, rather than stress, conflict, or drain us of our emotional energy.

Will reading this book guarantee that you'll be able to navigate all your difficult relationships? Not necessarily—there are no guarantees. However, it will provide you with greater clarity about the people in your life, helping you to better understand their behavior and how it affects you. This awareness will empower you to approach these relationships with more understanding and know which ones you can safely dedicate your time to.

My wife used to spend countless hours on the phone with this particular woman who was draining our emotional energy. When I expressed my concern about how much time she was dedicating, she said it was a good deed to support someone going through emotional turmoil. She may have been right—helping others is admirable, but when someone's turmoil drags on for years without them making any effort to change, it's worth questioning whether continuing to help is truly beneficial, especially for those spending their precious time to help them.

People aren't like dishwashers—you can't just call a repairman to replace a heating element and expect them to function properly again. Emotional issues often take years of therapy to come to terms with them and heal. The challenge here is that my wife isn't a therapist, and when someone needs a lot more energy than you are willing to give, it can strain other relationships.

Recognizing when someone is draining your energy is crucial. It's not always healthy—or even helpful—to continue pouring yourself into someone who requires more support than you're able or willing to give. Learning to set boundaries can help ensure that your efforts to support others don't come at the expense of your own well-being or the health of your other relationships.

My ultimate goal for this book is to help you build a life filled with healthy relationships; the kind where your circle of friends and relatives are the ones that bring you joy. At the same time, you'll learn how to manage the ones who drain your energy without letting them destroy your inner serenity. When more of us learn how to do that, the world will be much happier—and so will you.

Categories of Emotional Vampires

A vampire is a legendary creature that survives by feeding on the blood of the living. In European folklore, these undead beings were said to rise from their graves, returning to haunt loved ones and wreak havoc in their former communities—spreading fear, mischief, and even death.

Just as a vampire sucks you of your blood, an Emotional Vampire is someone who sucks the energy out of you and causes you to be emotionally drained. Who wants to go through life constantly being drained by the dysfunction of other people, or even causing other people to be drained by you? The only thing I want to suck on are spicy chicken wings.

We are going to define many categories of personality traits that may be causing this trauma in your life. These are the people whose name you dread seeing in a text notification, on your calendar, or on a guest list. You may be in a relationship with them, they may be a co-worker or friend, but more often than not, they're family: a parent, sibling, or relative you feel obligated to engage with. And don't be surprised; if someone fits into one category, there's a good chance they'll show up in a few others too. Emotional dysfunction rarely travels alone.

Emotional Vampires can be as tame as someone who talks too much—Non-Stop Talkers, to an insidious group far more toxic, like The Projectors—those who spend a lifetime accusing you of the very things they've done to you. From mildly annoying to emotionally destructive, they all have one thing in common: they leave you feeling utterly drained.

Just to be clear, you may even be an Emotional Vampire yourself. Although many will refuse to accept this, you will find that coming to terms with this will make your life a lot happier and your relationships healthier.

Recognizing who in your life is an Emotional Vampire and who's a Keeper brings powerful clarity. The people you surround yourself with are one of the strongest predictors of your emotional well-being.

This doesn't mean you have to cut all the vampires out of your life, but it does mean you need to set healthy boundaries and protect your happiness. Knowing the difference isn't about judgment—it's about survival.

Let's be real—Emotional Vampires come in all shapes and sizes. The following are some of the usual suspects. This isn't a complete list because that would take volumes. These are the ones I've personally survived—and chances are, you've met a few of them too.

Grab some garlic. Here we go.

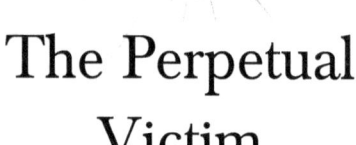

The Perpetual Victim

"They've never met a problem that wasn't someone else's fault."

These are people who love to play the victim card. You can also call them Injustice Collectors. They love to let people know how they're getting the short end of the stick in life. They often blame their misfortune on others and will try to drag you down to their pessimistic level when you're with them. These individuals perpetually see themselves as helpless victims of circumstances, refusing to take responsibility for their lives or make meaningful changes. These are people who find it more convenient to shift the blame, clinging to their role as helpless victims.

Case Study: *A woman in her mid-30s who had been attending my classes once approached me after a session, clearly overwhelmed by the challenges she was facing. After class, it's not uncommon for a small group to linger, hoping for a few minutes of guidance. And while ten minutes isn't much, I've learned that a little insight often goes a long way.*

She began sharing the weight of her past decade; ten years spent caring for her aging father back in England. She and her brother had bought a house together, but somehow, despite paying half the mortgage, he had managed to push her out. To make matters worse, her sisters were now trying to control her access to their father. The sheer volume of pain and family conflict she poured out in those few minutes was overwhelming; a lifetime of stress in a single conversation.

Her core complaint was the emotional toll her family was taking on her. I gently suggested that the first step to regaining control was to take ownership of her life. Build financial independence and consider creating some distance from the toxic environment that was draining her.

She kept circling back to blame; replaying every injustice, focusing entirely on what her family had done to her.

Eventually, I asked her a direct and necessary question: "Do you truly want help—or are you more committed to collecting injustices and staying stuck in the blame game?"

No matter how many times I encouraged her to take responsibility for her own life, she kept defaulting to the same role; the Perpetual Victim, blaming everyone else for her pain.

Eventually, after several weeks of attending my classes and hearing the same message repeated from different angles, something finally clicked.

She got a job.

She moved to a new city. And when she reached out to me later, her voice was lighter. She was happier, and finally in control of her own life, instead of being controlled by her family.

In situations such as this, sometimes the person has such animosity that they can't even see that they may have a victim mentality.

Victim mentality is a psychological mindset where a person consistently sees themselves as a victim of the negative actions of others, even when there's little or no objective evidence to support it. People with a victim mentality often believe:

- Bad things always happen to them, and they have no control over their lives.

- Others are to blame for their problems or unhappiness.

- Life is unfair, and they're singled out for mistreatment or misfortune.

- They deserve sympathy rather than having to be accountable or search for solutions.

This mindset can be a defense mechanism—sometimes rooted in real past trauma or unfair treatment, but when it becomes a pattern, it can lead to:

- Avoidance of responsibility
- Chronic complaining
- Difficulty maintaining relationships
- Resistance to any change

It's important to note that having a victim mentality doesn't mean someone isn't suffering, but staying in that mental state can keep someone stuck, instead of empowering them to take back control of their life.

How do you overcome it or help someone else who's stuck in this mindset? Overcoming a victim mentality is absolutely possible and incredibly empowering. It's about shifting from feeling powerless to owning your own story. Here's some steps to move out of that victim mindset:

- Recognize the pattern because awareness is the first breakthrough. Ask yourself: Do I often blame others for my situation? Do I feel stuck, helpless, or resentful most of the time? Write down your thoughts when something upsets you. See if there's a recurring theme of blame or powerlessness.

- Take radical responsibility. You can't control what happens to you, but you can control how you respond to it.

- Try saying: "This happened to me, but now I choose what happens next."

- Practice gratitude. Each day, list 3 things you're grateful for.
- Surround yourself with empowering people because the victim mentality can be reinforced by negative people in your lives. Connect with people who take ownership of their lives.

True change only happens when someone is ready to take control of their own life. It's only then that they can begin to forgive others for the harm they caused. If you continue living in a cycle of blame, constantly pointing fingers at other people, you'll only keep facing the same struggles. Taking ownership of your life is the key to breaking free.

Many times, The Perpetual Victim will exploit the court system, attempting to sue their way out of their own problems. While some lawsuits are valid, many simply shift blame onto others for issues they themselves have caused.

There are individuals who spend their entire lives entangled in legal battles, pinning their success on the outcome of a lawsuit rather than accept accountability. Some lawyers even build their careers around claims of wrongful termination, capitalizing on a culture that increasingly avoids personal responsibility. We seem to live in a society that often prioritizes litigation over self-reflection of one's shortcomings

Some people simply cannot move forward in life knowing they've been wronged or have made poor decisions. This is especially true in financial matters, whether it's buying when you should have sold or selling when patience would have led to a better opportunity.

I live with a mantra that helps me let go when I find myself on the losing end of a situation: You may be right, but that doesn't mean you always get to win.

Case study: *Back in 2010, I discovered a company called Sodastream, which operated under the "blade and razor" business model—named after Gillette's strategy of selling razors at a low cost while making recurring profits from disposable blades. Similarly, once a customer bought a Sodastream machine, they were locked into purchasing CO2 cartridges, which needed regular replacement. The company held a patent that ensured the cartridges were safe and easy to use, allowing customers to swap them at local grocery stores.*

I saw this as a brilliant business model. After all, who enjoys lugging heavy bottles of soda water from the store when they could simply make it at home? Beyond convenience, my investment thesis had additional strengths. The soda industry is massive, and growing environmental concerns were pushing for a reduction in single-use plastic bottles. In eco-conscious cities like San Diego and Portland, it seemed plausible that plastic bottles might even be banned, forcing major soda brands to adapt by offering their syrups for home use.

My thesis was partially correct. In 2018, Pepsi acquired Sodastream for $3.2 billion. However, despite being right about the company's potential, I didn't profit as much as I could have. My mistake? Instead of buying and holding the stock, I focused on options contracts, which lost value as they approached expiration. While I did own some *shares, I would have made a small fortune if I had simply invested in the stock and been patient. It was a classic case of being right, but not winning.*

It would have been easy to blame the company, bad luck, or external factors for my missed opportunity. Instead, I chose to take the small win and, more importantly, I learned two key lessons:

1. If I believe a company is likely to be acquired, the best strategy is to buy the stock, hold it, and let time work in my favor.
2. Sometimes you're right and you still don't win—and that's okay, as long as you learn from it.

Unfortunately, I encounter many people who come from emotionally unhealthy families. Is it their fault they ended up in that environment? Absolutely not. But healing isn't about fault—it's about responsibility. To move forward, they must seek professional help and take ownership of their lives.

The first and most crucial step? Forgive the source of their pain.

That doesn't mean excusing the harm—it means releasing its grip. Because as long as they continue to blame others, even if the blame is justified, they'll remain emotionally stuck. True healing only begins when the cycle of blame ends.

Otherwise, they risk becoming an Emotional Vampire—not just to those around them, but tragically, to themselves.

Sometimes, we have to adopt the same mindset I had when trying to predict the Sodastream buyout—you can be right… and still not win.

You might pick the right stock, but mistime the market. You might come up with a brilliant idea—and watch someone else profit from it. You might score the most points in a basketball game—and still lose. You might marry someone who seemed perfect—until they turn into someone you can't stand. You might eat healthy, exercise daily—and still get an incurable disease. You might never miss a class, pull all-night study sessions and still walk away with a B minus.

Life isn't fair.

And the sooner you stop believing that you're owed something better, the freer and more content you'll be. Because chasing fairness will only keep you bitter. But accepting reality? That's where peace begins.

God doesn't always give you what you want—He gives you what you need. Every challenge you face isn't just an obstacle; it's a tool meant to shape you, teach you, and strengthen you.

The moment you shift your mindset from "Why me?" to "What's next?" is the moment you begin to take ownership of your mental and emotional well-being.

You have a choice: keep blaming people, circumstances, timing, luck—or move forward.

You can't control other people. You can only control your reactions to them. And that's where your real power begins.

An Emotional Vampire isn't always just a person—it can be a collective mindset. Sometimes entire groups adopt a victim mentality, constantly blaming external forces for their misfortunes instead of taking responsibility for their future.

It drains energy and keeps everyone stuck in the same cycle.

The United States has long stood as a beacon of opportunity—a place where hard work and perseverance can transform poverty into a comfortable life. This promise has drawn immigrants from every corner of the globe, many arriving with nothing but hope and determination.

Consider the Koreans, Chinese, Jews, Italians, and many other Europeans who came to America during the Industrial Revolution with almost nothing. Within just a generation or two, they built thriving businesses and strong families, proving that success is possible through resilience and effort. Meanwhile, some groups remain trapped in a cycle of blame, attributing their struggles to injustices from a century ago rather than focusing on the opportunities available today. Growth begins when we shift our focus from what was done to us—to what we can do now.

While history undeniably shapes the present, the most successful individuals recognize that progress comes not from dwelling on the past, but from taking charge of the future.

Blaming is draining—usually served with a generous side of complaining. And let's be honest: that's not the kind of person we want to be, or be around. It takes real love, patience, and emotional maturity to walk with someone through their drama without getting pulled into it. When that support is rooted in love and compassion—something powerful happens.

You don't feel drained. You feel uplifted.

Because instead of feeding the chaos, you're helping them rise from it. And in that space of empathy and growth, they start to bury the Emotional Vampire within—and begin taking ownership of their own life.

> *"Blaming is draining—usually served with a generous side of complaining"*

Don't be a prisoner to your anger

In the book The Choice, by Auschwitz survivor Edith Eger, she shares stories of how upon liberation, many survivors walked out of the gates of the camps. Surprisingly, many of them also walked right back into the camps. Just because we are physically free, does not mean we are emotionally free.

Our neural pathways can be strong and they can keep us from forgetting or forgiving the past. The only real way to free yourself of this mental jail is to find the source—whoever or whatever circumstance happened that caused you to stay in an emotional prison.

Why is understanding the source important to your self-esteem? Because once you can figure it out, you will know what steps to take to cure it. However, the most important thing is to forgive the source of your low self-esteem. Constantly blaming others for your challenges will just turn you into a Perpetual Victim who just collects injustices for themselves; that is not the kind of collector you want to be.

The Narcissist

*"Mirror, Mirror on Every Wall,
Oh How I Love to See Them Fall."*

Out of all the categories of Emotional Vampires, this one may be the most menacing. It's dangerous because you have no idea what's lurking behind someone's charming personality. If it is a friend of yours, you can manage it because in all likelihood, they are a friend of convenience, or you like being drama adjacent. If the narcissist is your boss or co-worker, then there are tools where you can survive their attempts at manipulating you.

If they are your spouse, then you need to learn ways in which to confront it on a daily basis. Major therapy will be needed in order for that marriage to work, that is, unless you're both narcissists, in which case... good luck out-narcissi-zing each other.

Unfortunately, it is almost impossible for a narcissist to admit to themselves that they need therapy.

Narcissistic Personality Disorder (NPD) is a psychological condition marked by an intense need for attention and admiration, often at the expense of others. People with NPD have a distorted sense of self-importance and a striking lack of empathy. To maintain their inflated self-image, they may resort to manipulative, controlling, or even abusive behaviors to get what they want.

The scary part?

People with NPD can be incredibly charming and charismatic. Their magnetic personality draws others in easily making it all too easy to overlook the red flags until you're already entangled.

The word narcissist comes from ancient Greek mythology, where a handsome figure named Narcissus became so captivated by his own reflection in a pool of water that he couldn't look away, eventually wasting away in self-adoration.

Have you ever noticed how a mirror in a shopping mall has the gravitational pull of a black hole for passing teenagers?

It's no wonder there is a popular joke: "How do you drown a narcissist? Put a mirror at the bottom of a pool."

Healthy relationships are built on reciprocity, but narcissists struggle with that. They take, but rarely give back in a meaningful way. That's why if you ended up marrying a narcissist, there's a good chance you got trapped.

What makes them dangerous is how easy it is to get pulled in. Their charm is disarming, their confidence magnetic, but beneath the surface, they're masters of deception. Spend enough time with a narcissist, and you'll notice something unsettling: you barely spoke and they barely listened.

Some typical traits of narcissists:

- Charismatic
- Needs to be admired and the center of attention
- Have a preoccupation with power
- Preoccupied with their looks (aren't we all?)
- Envious of others or think others are envious of them
- Feel entitled
- Can be manipulative (gaslighting)
- Lacks empathy
- Difficulties with long term relationships
- Fragile self-esteem
- Lacks accountability
- Inflates their achievements
- Difficulty respecting boundaries

Defining Terms

The word narcissist gets thrown around a lot these days. But when powerful terms are overused or misapplied, they begin to lose their meaning. We've seen this happen with words like Holocaust or genocide—terms that should describe unimaginable atrocities, but are sometimes used to label any violent conflict. In many cases, the more accurate word would simply be war. When we dilute the language this way, these words lose their weight, and with that, their ability to truly convey the gravity of the situations they were meant to describe.

I've touched on this same issue in my public classes when discussing the word "love." We use it so broadly—it describes our feelings for a romantic partner, our parents, siblings, school, dog, and even our favorite slice of pizza. When one word stretches to cover so many different kinds of affection, it starts to lose its clarity and depth.

It's fascinating that the Inuit people of Northern Canada have over 50 words to describe snow, even though it is all based on the same word. And it makes sense—when you live in the north, you quickly realize that not all snow is the same. Some is perfect for sledding, some packs well for snowballs, some melts the moment it touches the ground, and some turns roads into slippery hazards.

I sometimes wonder why we only have one word for love. Sure, we use words like adore, enjoy, cherish, admire, care for, and prize, but none of them quite capture the same depth—or breadth—of what we mean by love. After all, you probably wouldn't say you admire a slice of mushroom pizza. You might adore your dog or care for a sibling, but when those words don't feel strong enough, we default to love. It's our catch-all for everything from deep emotional bonds to fleeting pleasures—and that may be part of the problem.

The love we feel for a spouse is nothing like the love we feel for our mom—unless your marriage is really weird—yet we use the same word for both. That's the trouble with language; when we use one label for very different experiences, meanings get blurred. The same goes for the term narcissist. These days, it's often used to describe anyone who's selfish, self-centered, or emotionally unavailable. But there's a big difference between someone with narcissistic tendencies and someone with full-blown NPD. Still, for the purpose of this book, the distinction doesn't matter all that much—because regardless of where they fall on the spectrum, one thing is clear; they leave you emotionally drained and wondering if you're the crazy one.

False Devotion Though Oxytocin

There's a fascinating theory that people with NPD may have impaired production of oxytocin—the hormone often nicknamed the "love hormone" or "cuddle chemical." Oxytocin is naturally produced in the brain and plays a key role in human behavior, especially bonding, trust, and emotional connection. It gets released when we hug, touch, or emotionally connect with someone, and it increases with each bonding moment. This is why mothers create such strong attachments to their babies—and why babies instinctively bond right back. In healthy relationships, oxytocin helps glue people together.

But here's the kicker: if someone's brain doesn't produce enough oxytocin, those warm fuzzy feelings just don't show up to the party. That's why bonding with a narcissist can feel like hugging a cactus—no matter how many times you try, it's prickly, unrewarding, and you're the one who ends up bloody.

There may be some truth to this, as people with NPD often fail to produce this hormone. But here's the deeper issue: most people think of love as a feeling. They say, "I feel like I'm in love," usually because they're overwhelmed with the desire to give, to care, to connect—without expecting anything in return.

That kind of love, while beautiful, is not enough to sustain a long-term relationship. It treats love as a noun—a thing you fall into or out of—rather than a verb, something you are actively doing. It's not something that just happens to you like the flu or that warm fuzzy thing you get when someone shares their fries. That's infatuation... or maybe just hunger.

Real, lasting love isn't just something you feel; it's something you do. Love should be an action word. It does the dishes. It listens even when it's tired—even when you don't *feel* like it.

That warm, generous feeling we call "being in love"—where you just want to give without expecting anything in return—can actually be a trap, especially if a narcissist catches the scent. Because the moment they sniff out someone who loves to give, they latch on to them. Then the unsuspecting giver soon falls head over heels, and before they realize what's happening, the unsuspecting nice person is having their vulnerability stepped on as often as you get free samples at Costco. Meanwhile, the narcissist is doing backflips inside, thinking, "Jackpot."

Yes, the oxytocin is flowing—but it's a one-way street. The giver is flooded with bonding chemicals; the narcissist, meanwhile, is just enjoying the perks: attention, admiration, and free emotional room service. This is how narcissists gain the upper hand—they exploit people whose default setting is generosity and empathy. It's like showing up to a poker game thinking you're just playing in a checkers tournament… and the other person puts you all-in—not with poker chips, but your heart!

Gaslighting is Not So Exciting

Gaslighting is one of the narcissist's favorite party tricks—although they don't have exclusive rights to it, narcissists take it to Olympic levels. They'll flat-out deny things they said five minutes ago—while you're still holding the text message. They'll make you feel "crazy" for seeing things the way you do and twist facts like they're auditioning for a job on The Daily Show. The goal? Control. Slowly, you start to question your memory, your perception, even your sanity. Before you know it, you don't even notice until you're halfway through apologizing for something they did… while bringing them a snack.

Before long, you're second-guessing your memory, your instincts, and maybe even your mental-health.

The term gaslighting comes from a 1938 play called Gas Light, where a manipulative husband tries to drive his wife insane by subtly dimming the lights in their home. When she notices and questions it, he insists nothing has changed—making her doubt her own sanity. It's a textbook example of psychological manipulation.

The Real You Isn't So Real

One of the most painful parts of being in a narcissistic marriage is that no one else sees the narcissist for who they really are. To friends, coworkers, and even extended family, they come across as charming, generous, and put-together. Meanwhile, behind closed doors, you're drowning in emotional chaos. This leaves the victim feeling isolated—like they're stranded on an island where no one believes their version of reality. The narcissist causes the damage, then points to your reaction as the problem. "See? You're the crazy one." That makes healing so much harder, because it feels like the whole world is rooting for your abuser.

It's like everyone else is watching the highlight video, and you're stuck in the blooper reel and there's no laugh track.

When phrases like "You owe me," "You're such a tease," or "Relax, I was just kidding" start popping up, congratulations—you're no longer in a relationship… you're in a manipulation-ship.

After the narcissist says something hurtful, they'll double down with silence or the cold shoulder. And what happens next? The victim ends up apologizing just to smooth things over... even though they didn't do anything wrong. Why? Because keeping the illusion of a healthy relationship feels easier than confronting reality.

If someone keeps giving and giving but never gets anything in return, the relationship is eventually going to collapse. At first, the giver doesn't notice, because they like giving. It feels good and it feels like love, but over time, they start to realize something's off... like, "Wait a minute—why am I emotionally broke and they're not?" That's usually when the lightbulb goes off: this might not be mutual... this might be narcissism. But by the time the giver figures it out, the giver's exhausted, confused, and wondering where their self-esteem wandered off to.

This is why it is hard for people to recognize narcissist tendencies early on in a relationship. It is only once you realize that you are always giving and not receiving anything in return that you may be emotionally tied to a narcissist. By that point, it's not just a relationship—it's a subscription you forgot to cancel, and now it's auto-renewing in emotional pain.

Narcissists love drama and feed off of emotional reactions. But if there's one thing they love, that's flattery. Compliments are their emotional currency—tell them they're brilliant, and they'll light up like a kid in a candy store. If you're smart and a little strategic, you can actually use this to your advantage—especially in business.

Case study: I once worked with a business associate who was extremely difficult. Every interaction felt like walking on eggshells. However, he consistently sold me deals, so maintaining the relationship was advantageous and something I did not want to give up.

Over time, I realized that his behavior was driven largely by ego and the need for validation. Rather than confront him directly, I adjusted my approach. I made an effort to compliment him, especially in front of other people.

This small shift changed everything. He became easier to work with. In fact, not only did our working relationship improve, but he also started bringing me more business. The experience taught me that understanding someone's emotional drivers—even if they're rooted in narcissistic tendencies—can be the key to managing them effectively.

It's only when you step back and view the bigger picture, using your intelligence instead of your emotions, that you begin to understand why people behave the way they do. That's when you can start turning someone's flaws into a strategic advantage.

We see this even at the highest levels of diplomacy, where skilled individuals use another person's flaw to influence someone else, making themselves more persuasive.

Case study: A few weeks after President Trump ordered strikes on Iran's nuclear facilities, Prime Minister Benjamin Netanyahu visited the White House. During the meeting, he presented President Trump with a letter he had sent to the Nobel Peace Prize Committee—recommending Trump for the award.

It was a masterclass in emotional intelligence: understanding someone's core drives, and in this case, recognizing President Trump's desire to leave a legacy of peace making.

The "It was a Joke" Narcissist

This type of narcissist delivers a cutting or inappropriate remark—then hides behind the phrase, "It was just a joke." On the surface, it may sound harmless, but this tactic serves several deeper (and more toxic) purposes:

- Deflection: If you call them out, they act as though you're the problem—for not having a sense of humor. By framing it as a joke, they avoid taking responsibility for their words or actions.

- Manipulation: This move also works as a form of emotional manipulation. If you feel hurt, you're made to believe you're overreacting or being "too sensitive." The goal is to make you second-guess your own emotional response—classic gaslighting.

Bottom line: When a narcissist says, "It was just a joke," it's rarely about humor. It's usually about control. Their comfort takes precedence over your emotional safety, and the joke becomes a tool for dismissal, not connection.

This is the danger that a narcissist will create. Completely hidden from you until you have already taken the bait.

Other Signs of Narcissism

- They control the relationship like a director on set—you just follow the script. Things are "good" when they say so, and suddenly "bad" when they decide. Your needs, feelings, and voice are sidelined. Over time, you begin to feel like a background character in your own life, with little control over your happiness or stability.

- You have a fear of losing them, even when you know you should. Despite the pain they cause, the thought of losing them is terrifying. You obsess over the relationship, even though your friends have practically staged an intervention. They lie, manipulate, and erode your confidence, but somehow, you still feel like you need them. The worse they treat you, the more they chip away at your self-worth, making it even harder to leave.

- You have crippling low self-esteem. Your sense of self becomes so distorted that if someone asked you to name three positive things about yourself, you'd struggle. Why? Because your identity is now based on what they think of you. Your self-esteem is no longer self-generated—it's outsourced to your abuser. The more they tear you down, the more you believe them. It's a vicious cycle that's incredibly difficult to break without help.

What do narcissists mean when they say the following:

I love you

What they mean: I love having control over you. I can sweet-talk you and get pleasure from using you. It feels great to shower you with love at first, then drop you whenever I want. When I flatter you, I can get anything I want. You trust me and open up easily, even after I've hurt you. Once you're invested in me, I'll make you fall just to watch you get hurt.

I am sorry you feel that way

What they mean: I'm not really sorry. I just want to end this argument so I can keep acting badly without worry. I'm not sorry for what I did; I'm only sorry I got caught. I don't care about your feelings because I believe I deserve everything, no matter how it affects you.

You're oversensitive/overreacting

What they mean: You're reacting normally to the awful things I'm doing, but I see that you're starting to catch on. I'll make you doubt yourself (gaslighting) so you keep accepting my behavior. As long as you don't trust yourself, you'll work hard to make excuses for me while I benefit without facing any consequences.

You're crazy

What they mean: I enjoy causing chaos to make you react. When you do, I can say you're the one with problems. No one will believe you if they think you're just bitter or unstable, when in reality, you are being gaslighted. In the end, I just want to look superior.

My exes are crazy

What they mean: I made my exes seem crazy. It was easy! I would provoke them until they reacted, and then I used those reactions to make them look unhinged. Soon, you'll be the "crazy ex" too.

No one would believe you

What they mean: I've isolated you, so you feel like you have no support. I've told lies about you to others, so they suspect the worst about you. Some people won't believe you, especially those who still think I'm a great person and support me.

Do you have an empathetic personality? If so, you're basically shark bait to a narcissist. But who's even more likely to end up in an abusive relationship than someone who's just empathetic? Someone who's empathetic and has low self-esteem. Now we're talking shark bait covered in fresh blood, waving a little flag that says, "Please exploit me!" Narcissists can sniff out that combo like Joey Chestnut can find an all-you-can-eat hot dog buffet. You're kind, giving, and always trying to see the best in others—exactly the traits that make you irresistible... to the very person who will take you for everything you've got.

The defining trait of an empath is the ability to deeply understand and feel other people's emotions. If you've ever wondered why strangers seem to open up to you about their problems—or why friends treat you like their personal therapist—it's probably because you're an empath. Empaths tend to be more emotionally sensitive than most, often picking up on moods, tension, and unspoken feelings in a room without anyone saying a word.

But that sensitivity comes with a cost. Because empaths are often emotionally open and unguarded, their feelings are more easily hurt. It doesn't take much for someone to step on their emotions—sometimes without even realizing it. And unfortunately, narcissists have a radar for this kind of vulnerability.

The Narcissist Sniff Test

If you're in a relationship with someone and unsure whether they might be a narcissist, these questions can help you gain clarity and spot the warning signs early.

Ask them if they love you.

When they say yes (and they probably will), follow up with, "Why do you love me?" If you're possibly dealing with a narcissist, pay close attention to the answer—because it will likely revolve around them.

You might hear things like:

"I love you because you love me."

"I love you because you pulled me out of a dark place."

"I love you because you make me laugh."

Notice the pattern? It's all about what you do for them, or how you make them feel. What you likely won't hear are statements that reflect your actual character—like, "I love you because you're kind, strong, or thoughtful." In a narcissist's version of love, you are just a supporting actor in their movie. The "love" they claim to feel isn't really about you—it's about how well you follow their script.

If the person you're dating has been married more than once, ask about their exes.

If every single one is labeled as "crazy," that's not a coincidence—it's a red flag the size of the state of Texas. We've all had a few rough relationships, but if every ex is allegedly unstable, dramatic, or impossible, the common denominator might not be the exes—it might be them. Chances are, those exes weren't born "crazy." They may have been driven there—slowly—by being gaslit, devalued, ignored, dismissed, used, abused, belittled, let down, cheated on, invalidated, minimized, made to feel invisible, and blamed for everything. That kind of emotional warfare will dismantle anyone's identity, self-worth, and confidence over time.

So if all their exes are nuts… you might be next on that list.

Ask them if they have taken any responsibility for a failed relationship.

Now pay close attention—not just to what they say, but how they respond. If any of the following happens, consider it a flashing warning sign:

- They get defensive or angry
- They dodge the question entirely
- They blame or trash their ex ("She was unstable… he was impossible…")

- They twist the question into something else entirely
- They suddenly need to end the conversation

These are emotional exit signs. A healthy person can reflect on the past and own their part in it. Narcissists struggle to admit they're anything less than perfect—so when you question their perspective or suggest that they might share some responsibility, they deflect instead of reflect. They cast themselves as the victim, and leave everyone else holding the blame.

Ask them to do you a favor.

If they know they're not going to get anything out of it from you, or use it to hold against you later, they'll promise and yet still blow it off and make excuses—"I forgot", "I was out of gas", "my goldfish died", etc…

Ask them to do something else that you'd enjoy more.

If they suggest doing something they're interested in instead, that's a red flag. Narcissists tend to get bored or distracted quickly when things aren't going their way. If they seem disinterested the moment the spotlight shifts off of them, it's a sign you're not in a partnership—you're in a one-person show where you've accidentally wandered onto the stage.

Here is a great test to see someone's capacity for empathy:

Yawn in front of them and watch what happens. Most people will instinctively follow suit. It's not just social mimicry—it's the brain's empathy circuits kicking in. Like reaching for your drink at a dinner table and suddenly everyone else does the same, we unconsciously mirror those around us.

But narcissists? They don't yawn back. Not because they're immune to boredom, but because they're often missing the very wiring that triggers that empathetic response. It's a subtle, science-backed tell. If you notice during this test that you're yawning alone, you're probably better off *being* alone.

Tips on How to Deal with A Narcissist

Don't play their game. It's a game with the odds stacked against you. If you are not feeding their ego or giving them praise, they will try to provoke a reaction from you and get you upset because they delight in your frustration just as much as they delight in your praise. It looks beatable, but it's not. We are better off saying less and keeping our comments to a minimum. Say things that are neutral like:

- I'll have to think about that
- Noted
- I can see that
- That's good to know

We want to stay as neutral in our conversations as possible. Our greatest tool is silence because no one can argue with, misquote or manipulate silence.

They do anything to empower their reputation and image. So instead of getting frustrated or trying to convince them of how they made you feel, flip the switch ask for what you want in a way that benefits them or their reputation.

You can't negotiate with their ego, but you can navigate around it.

Narcissists aren't looking for compromise, they are looking for control. You can flip the script by using tactical empathy. Say, "This seems like this is really important to you." It makes them feel validated without you having to agree with anything they are saying.

If a narcissist says to you, "If you don't do this, I am going to have to work 10 extra hours next week"—in this situation, it's not about the hours, it's about guilt.

Respond with, "I know you didn't mean to do it, but you made me feel guilty about you having to work next week. I know you're a good person and you didn't intend to mean it that way." Always call it out, but do it in a non-confrontational way and always give them an out.

In the ancient classic, The Art of War, this tactic is known as building a Golden Bridge—giving your opponent a dignified way to retreat. Instead of cornering them, you offer an exit that protects their pride. The same applies when dealing with a narcissist: always leave them a way out that lets them save face. It's not surrender—it's strategy.

If a Narcissist Was Honest

This following is a conversation between 2 people on a first date[1]

---

1 Jimmy On Relationships, Instagram

Man: Hey! It's great to meet you.

Woman: Thank you so much.

Man: So, I'm a narcissist.

Woman: You seem so nice (as she spits water out of her mouth).

Man: Oh yeah, but I'm just pretending. I figured out if I'm charming and funny and give you lots of attention and affection, then I can get you to fall in love with me.

Woman: Why do you need me to fall in love with you?

Man: Because you're less likely to leave once I start lying and belittling and gaslighting you and chipping away at your self-worth in order to control and manipulate you. It works particularly well if you have a history of trauma, when you tend to blame yourself even though you're the one being neglected.

Woman: That sounds like abuse.

Man: Oh, it definitely is!

Woman: Why would you do that?

Man: Oh, I'm deeply insecure.

Woman: I can see that

Man: I have a massively fragile ego and fear of rejection so I've created a fantasy world in which I'm the center of the universe and everyone else is inferior.

Woman: Wow! Thanks for alerting me to this up front before we formed a complicated trauma bond that would have caused me years of misery!

Man: Well, I just want people to know what they are getting themselves into. I mean you don't by chance struggle with boundaries and self-esteem issues, do you?

Woman: I do actually.

Man: Dang it! We would have made a great pair I bet.

Woman: Good thing you showed me these red flags up front so I could protect myself.

Man: Well, if there's one thing, I am up front and transparent in the beginning.

If you sense a narcissist in your midst…run away!

Seriously, sprint. You're better off dealing with the next category of Emotional Vampire. Sure, they might trap you in a four-hour saga about how the Starbucks barista ruined their Frappuccino… but at least they won't dismantle your self-esteem in the process.

The Drama Queen

*"Lots of emotion
leads to mental erosion"*

These are the people who treat life like a reality show—and their social media feed is the highlight reel. They overshare like it's a sport. One minute they're surviving "the worst day ever" because their latte had almond milk instead of oat, and the next, they're posting a 37-photo slideshow from the most amazing weekend ever! (Usually with many exclamation points!!!!!!!!) They don't just experience life, they broadcast it with a flair for exaggeration that turns the ordinary into the outrageous.

Subtlety isn't their strong suit, but drama? They majored in it.

The weather is the worst ever, the traffic is always a nightmare, and their dates are always unacceptable. If there's no drama in the moment, don't worry—they'll create some.

It might be the co-worker who spends hours at the water cooler sharing every wild detail of their weekend adventures. These folks aren't dangerous—if anything, they're perfect for those who like to be drama-adjacent. You don't want their chaos, just the highlight reel. It's like living vicariously through someone else's rollercoaster while sitting safely in the stands.

This is often the married guy who works alongside a single colleague with a never-ending supply of dating stories—he gets the entertainment without having to swipe right himself.

Drama follows these people wherever they go—whether it's in their relationships, work, or daily interactions. They thrive on chaos and often pull you into their whirlwind of emotional highs and lows.

Case study: A friend of ours texted me about a woman who was coming to our town to perform a one-woman show and needed a place to eat lunch. Her show had been winning awards, and I was told she was incredibly talented. She was in her late 40s and really wanted to get married.

She asked if she could bring a friend along, and I said sure. Then she added, "She's a big influencer—way bigger than me." I told her I didn't care if her friend was an influencer or not—just make sure she doesn't have influenza. Honestly, someone's social media status has zero impact on whether I'm willing to host them for a meal.

As advertised, the actress was beautiful, charismatic, witty, and a lot of fun to be around. But I couldn't figure out why she was still single—until I realized she wasn't just a drama queen, she also wanted to be drama-adjacent. That likely explains why she thought her friend's influencer status was worth mentioning—it felt like she was drawn to people with big personalities, but also big followings.

While I genuinely enjoyed her company, I walked away thinking she's still single for one of two reasons: either she hasn't met a man who can bring enough drama to keep things exciting, or—more likely—she scares men off by constantly talking about how "big" everyone else is on social media. Most guys probably end up feeling like they're auditioning to be her supporting actor instead of her co-star.

Drama Queens may be candidates of having ADHD, Attention-Deficit Hyperactivity Disorder. They are the ones that are the most popular on social media. We all love them because they're fun, but sometimes they can be emotionally draining. When you're young, you love them because they bring attention to anyone near them. When you are older, you less likely need or want the attention, so you tend to stay away from them.

Case study: *I was walking outside my house in Jerusalem and I saw 2 women run into each other on the sidewalk.*

One said to the other, "When did you get here?" The other women responded, "We literally arrived this morning."

I thought to myself that this conversation may be a telltale sign of someone who is a Drama Queen.

Why else would someone need to throw in the word "literally?" The person who asked the woman when she arrived knew she lived overseas, so she obviously knew that she had to have arrived *sometime*. The woman should have answered, "We arrived this morning," instead of "we literally arrived this morning." The additional use of the word literarily was an unneeded emphasis. This may be someone who over emphasizes many other aspects of her life.

The word 'literally' should be used to emphasize something when what you are saying is true, although it seems exaggerated or shocking. There was nothing surprising or nothing to exaggerate about her arriving that morning.

Here is a true start and a good example of when to use the word *literally:*

A couple I'm very close with recently took a cruise and ended up sharing dinner each night with another couple they met onboard. Over the course of several evenings, they developed a nice rapport.

One night, while the two husbands were talking, the other man suddenly collapsed—right there at the dinner table—and died instantly.

When my friend told me the story afterward, he said, "I was talking to this guy, and he literally died at the table, right in front of me."

This is one of the rare moments where the word literally is used correctly. It wasn't for dramatic effect or exaggeration. It actually happened. He used the word not to be theatrical, but because it was the only word that truly fit the moment. Drama Queens use it because it creates more drama when they are speaking.

Case Study: A friend of mine used to attract a lot of attention at happy hours and singles events. He was extremely good-looking—the kind of guy who stirred up drama the moment he walked into a room. His friends loved tagging along, not because they were great wingmen, but because being around him meant catching the overflow of attention. In other words, they got the leftovers.

This last case is where being drama adjacent was a positive experience for those that liked hanging out with someone that created a lot of drama.

Other examples of someone being overly dramatic:

- Someone who over-analyzes's situations. You reply to a text with a "K" instead of "Okay." *Wow. Just 'K'? Are you mad at me? Are we breaking up?*

- Someone going through what they consider to be a wardrobe crisis, they can't find the right shoes to match their outfit. *"I have nothing to wear. Cancel the night. Cancel life."* If this is a man, then he probably is a Drama Queen (or a drama king). Also if a man is getting manicures, then most likely he is also over analyzing his outfits. You could make the argument that manicures *are specifically for men, s*ince many women trim and polish their own nails. Why else would it be called a *man-icure*?

- Someone who leaves a group chat with a dramatic exit message like: *"Good luck to all of you. I just can't anymore." (Returns quietly 12 hours later.)*

- The guilt tripping mom when her son did not come for dinner. *"No, it's fine. I'll just eat alone… again… like I did when you went off to college and forgot you had a mother."*

- "I guess I'm just invisible in this family."

- "Don't mind me, I'll just sit in the corner… like always."

Do you have any Drama Queens in your life? Do you find that it drains your energy when they are over dramatic? If so, you'll need to figure out how to make that relationship healthy. However, it may not be as bad as the next category of Emotional Vampires—they make Drama Queens look like emotional support animals.

The Socially Awkward

*"Uber Goobers are lovable...
preferably at someone else's party."*

You know those people at singles events who stand awkwardly in the corner, clutching a beer like it's a security blanket, completely unaware how to start a conversation? Yeah, you know the type—the ones your mom is always trying to set you up with.

Mom: "Stanley is so nice... why don't you give him a chance?"

Daughter: "Mom! He's a Super Uber Goober. He's not just awkward—he's got the social skills of a potted plant and the energy of a sock."

Mom: "He's just a little shy!"

Daughter: "He brought a yo-yo to the table and played with it during dinner. I don't care that he called it his icebreaker."

I cannot be the only one that gets emotionally drained from people that are socially awkward. My family seems to attract them to our dinner table very often on Friday nights. I can only handle so many conspiracy theories involving almond milk.

After having one of them attend a meal at my house, I dread the next time they text me asking to come for another meal.

"Had such a great time! Can I come again next week?"

I want to reply: *"Only if I'm not home."*

When we have a large group over for dinner, I'm much more inclined to say yes. It's because their social awkwardness can blend into the background noise of normal conversation. With enough people around, they become more of a footnote than the main event. I'll usually seat them at the far end of the table, safely out of range from my wife and me.

However, if it's a smaller, more intimate meal, I politely let them know we're keeping it just family that week. This is my diplomatic way of saying, "I need one dinner where I don't have to explain sarcasm or endure a 20-minute story about the cost of printer ink."

You can figure out pretty easily if someone is draining your emotional energy. When they leave your house, you feel a sense of relief and happiness. It is as if you feel a weight lifted off of your back. I am not insinuating that you should shun them from your social events, you just need to be aware so you can mentally prepare for them. These folks are everywhere! If someone insists they don't have any socially awkward people in their life? Let's be honest—it probably means they're the socially awkward one… and just haven't figured it out yet.

If you've ever been to a singles event, you've probably noticed: the number of socially awkward men far outweighs the number of socially awkward women. And I'm sure plenty of women can back me up on this.

It's not just anecdotal, there's data behind it. Males are diagnosed with Asperger's (now part of the autism spectrum) about four times more often than females. So yes, that guy nervously clinging to the snack table with stains on his shirt and talking non-stop about black holes? Statistically, he checks out.

I'm not suggesting that all socially awkward people have Asperger's. Just like someone can have narcissistic tendencies without having full-blown NPD, people can display traits commonly associated with Autism Spectrum Disorder, including Asperger's, without ever receiving a diagnosis. It's a spectrum for a reason, and many individuals fall somewhere along it without even realizing it.

Many of these men have no idea they're on the spectrum. While there may not be extensive data on this, I'd be willing to bet that a significant number of single men in their 40s and 50s would meet the criteria for some form of social or communication disorder, diagnosed or not.

They're not necessarily bad people, just socially unaware. And that lack of self-awareness is often what keeps them single.

Just like I tell men they can train themselves to become better listeners and remind women they can choose to find something to respect in their husbands, a socially awkward person can absolutely be coached out of being a full-blown weirdo in public.

Awkward isn't permanent. It's just an unrefined social muscle and like anything else, it can be strengthened with a little awareness, practice, and maybe someone gently saying, "Hey… maybe don't open your conversations with your top ten Dungeons and Dragons games of all time."

__Case Study:__ I met a nice young man recently—about 28 years old—who told me he was really ready to get married. So, like any good pseudo matchmaker, I invited him to one of our legendary Shabbat meals. We often host single men and women together—it's casual, low-pressure, and the only expectation is that you don't completely weird anyone out.

As we're all enjoying our soup, I glance over and notice our bachelor doing something I can only describe as not the best culinary choice: he picks up his bowl and slurps the last few drops like he's auditioning for a Japanese ramen noodle soup commercial. Now, to be fair—I've been known to do the same thing, but at home, alone, with the shades drawn.

The real showstopper came during the main course. He was eating chicken thighs, and instead of placing the bones neatly on a napkin, or what would have been better, to throw them away in the trash, he just started lining them up on the table. Like trophies. One by one. I half expected him to build a little bone fort by dessert.

He's a nice guy with a good heart, but no one ever taught him the basics of dinner table decency. I truly hope I get the chance to coach him.

That dinner inspired me to create a class called "From Swipe Right to Wedding Night: How to Make Yourself Irresistibly Marriageable." Now, maybe you'll read the book version one day, but before we get to becoming marriage material, let's talk about something just as important: how to handle awkward people without losing your appetite.

Socially awkward people can be absolutely brilliant. In fact, many of them used to hang out together in the high school computer club. These are the ones who were not-so-lovingly called geeks, nerds, or propeller heads.

Back then, no one from the cool crowd wanted to sit with them at lunch. Now those same guys are called Sergey Brin, Mark Zuckerberg, and Elon Musk. Turns out, the kids no one wanted to talk to are now the adults everyone wants to talk to!

There are many flavors of socially awkward. One of the most common is the "Know-It-All." This is the person who has an answer for everything, even when no one's asking. On the surface, they might seem brilliant. But remember:

Knowledge is knowing a tomato is a fruit.

Wisdom is knowing not to put it in a fruit salad.

The Know-It-All often blurs that line. They can impress people who aren't familiar with this particular brand of awkwardness, but beneath the surface, many are simply overcompensating. Interestingly, while some are genuinely intelligent, others may be masking learning disabilities or social struggles by clinging to useless facts.

There are many personality traits that can clue you in to whether someone is on the autism spectrum, including ones previously associated with Asperger's. I am only going to list the ones that I find easy to recognize:

- Has a hard time connecting to people in social situations
- Difficulty understanding social cues
- Difficulty understanding sarcasm and jokes
- Clumsy and awkward
- Has Emotional Constipation (lacking in emotional availability)

There's a valuable skill that socially awkward people are missing that could make interaction with them enjoyable and effort free. Psychologist Robert Sternberg calls it practical intelligence, one of three types of intelligence he identifies (the other two being analytical and creative). While analytical and creative intelligence are largely innate, practical intelligence is a skill you can develop. It's about knowing when and how to say things, understanding the nuances of situations, and responding thoughtfully. This type of intelligence helps you read situations accurately and have the social savvy to understand what you should, and shouldn't say to other people. Another way of saying it, using this skill will help you not to be a Super Uber Goober. Unfortunately, many socially awkward people do not recognize this, or if they do, they do not want to put the effort in to learn skills to act like a human being that does not have Emotional Constipation.

Case Study: I had a student who would often come over for meals. He was kind, soft-spoken, and always polite. Over time, I noticed he would ask the exact same questions during every visit: "How's the family? How's your wife? How's your son?" At first, I didn't think much of it. But eventually, it clicked—he was likely on the spectrum. I wouldn't be surprised if a therapist had coached him to ask those specific questions as a way to engage socially.

Is he my favorite dinner guest? Not exactly. But he's also not an Emotional Vampire. He's self-aware, respectful, and clearly doing the work to function well in social settings. And that effort earns a lot of credit in my book.

That experience taught me a valuable lesson: when someone is aware of their social awkwardness and makes the effort to compensate for it, they can navigate social situations without draining others.

Self-awareness, combined with intentional effort, can make even the most awkward person not only bearable—but even enjoyable to be around.

Case Study: *We had another frequent guest at our dinner table who, on his very first visit, told me he had Asperger's. He had a great voice, loved to sing, cracked corny jokes, and was always cheerful and eager to help clean up after dinner. Looking back, I realize that if he hadn't told me about his diagnosis upfront, I might not have been as patient—especially with the endless stream of dad-level jokes. But knowing where he was coming from gave me the perspective to appreciate his quirks rather than be irritated by them.*

That's why I believe it's so important for anyone who thinks they might be on the spectrum to seek support. With the right guidance, they can learn how to navigate social situations more smoothly and compensate for the areas where they may struggle. This particular guest ended up becoming one of my favorites. And honestly, I don't think I would've appreciated his presence if he hadn't been upfront about his condition. His honesty gave me the context I needed to understand and enjoy him for who he truly is.

Case study: *I met a man in one of my classes who was in his mid-40s and from my perspective, could use some help. You can sometimes tell right away when someone is socially awkward—not just by their appearance, but by their overall demeanor. He was one of those individuals who struggled in social settings. He confided in me about his difficulty getting a second date, and I empathized* *with his frustration, so I agreed to help. Unfortunately, as we worked together, his challenges proved to be even deeper than I initially realized.*

When we met for coffee, I noticed that he couldn't hold eye contact, constantly looking away as if searching into his mind for what to say next. It was like when someone giving a speech loses focus and glances upward to find their words—kind of like looking into their brain—except he did it nonstop, barely maintaining eye contact for more than a few seconds. I asked if he was aware of this habit, and he admitted he was, but had never attempted to do anything about it. I explained that on a date, if you can't keep eye contact with a woman, she's going to think you're nuts and you're unlikely to get a second chance. He seemed unaware that this was an issue. Unfortunately, he did nothing about it and is still having the same issues.

Sometimes the issues are so deeply ingrained that it takes an enormous amount of counseling just to bring them close to dateable.

Super Uber Goobers tend to stick together, mostly because no one else wants to hang out with them, except other socially awkward people. They'll often say other people are snobbish or stuck-up... and maybe there's a little truth to that.

The reality is, being around socially awkward people can be emotionally exhausting. Many of them unintentionally drain those around them, not out of malice, but because navigating a conversation with them feels like trying to solve a Rubik's cube with one hand.

I have always wondered if it is possible that I am the weirdo and everyone else that I consider to be awkward are the normal ones? That is just something to think about.

Emotional Constipation

*"Taking Ex-Lax for your feelings
has side effects that may include
honesty, connection,
and more bathroom breaks."*

There are marriages in which a man or woman chooses a partner who may be somewhat socially awkward. There's nothing inherently wrong with this. However, over time, they may come to realize that their partner is also emotionally constipated—unable or unwilling to open up emotionally and share their thoughts, feelings, joys, and sorrows.

Emotional constipation refers to the unhealthy habit of suppressing or holding back emotions, leading to a buildup of unprocessed feelings. This can manifest as difficulty expressing emotions and can lead to strained relationships. When emotions are not processed and expressed in healthy ways, they can even manifest as physical symptoms like digestive issues, or even emotional eating.

This is why people who are overweight aren't more hungry than the typical person. This cause of overeating is a physical manifestation of an emotional problem.

A partner in a marriage may have understood that their spouses inability to open up emotionally may have been an issue before they decided to marry them, it is only having lived with them for a number of years where it gets to be draining. Much worse than they could have ever imagined.

I don't want to beat up on the men, but from the circumstantial evidence that I have seen, this is more of an issue that men are challenged with.

This is not as much of a major issue if they are your friend, classmate, or business associate. Those relationships are more superficial. If you had a friend that is emotionally constipated, that emotional connection is not as strong as having a spouse, so it won't affect you that much.

The reason you got married—or want to get married—is to have a safe space where you can be vulnerable, share your feelings, and know you won't be judged or criticized. Emotional constipation isn't just the inability to express your own emotions—it can also mean being unable to receive or empathize with someone else's. When your partner is not emotionally available for you, it will drain you of your own emotional energy. A spouse needs someone to bounce their feelings off of—the need for someone to be a part of their emotional world. They need someone to understand them and have empathy for what they are going through.

You expect your spouse to be happy for you when you are happy, and to be sad for you when you are sad. If you can't be vulnerable with your spouse, this is a relationship doomed for failure. No one wants to be married to that kind of life sucking vampire. I hate to be so harsh in my verbiage, but that is what will happen when your spouse has Emotional Constipation.

A good listener is the key to avoiding this. Even if a partner is just *pretending* to listen, it will help tremendously. This means looking right at someone as they are talking to you and *not* looking anywhere else, at your phone or in the room.

It is often said that communication is the key to a great relationship. That is true, but what are the key aspects of communication? If you don't clarify what they are, you may be thinking that it is a couple talking through a tin can connected by a string. That's how we played "spy" when we were 10 years old back in the 1970's before walkie talkies became toys.

Healthy communication consists of two distinct parts. Affectionate speech from one party and effective listening from the other party. If you want to capture someone's attention and their heart, you have to use your ears properly. It is no coincidence, or it actually *is* a coincidence, that the word *heart* has the word *ear* right in the middle of it. So if someone is not listening properly, just as much as if someone is not speaking in an affectionate manner, communication will suffer along with the relationship.

Even if you know that your future spouse may not be the most socially adept, the lack of sharing *and* showing their emotions will lower the passion in a relationship. Seriously, if someone is not going to be emotionally available for you, you may as well marry a labradoodle. At least they will *always* be there to follow you around the house and lick you. However, if you need someone to take out the garbage, mop the floor, and clean the bathrooms, hire a maid—they are a heck of a lot cheaper than a spouse, and if you don't like them, you don't have to divorce them!

Even I have some issues with emotional constipation. Although I don't have a problem sharing my joy and enthusiasm, it is sadness that does not come so easy for me. When my father died, I did not cry, even though I had a tremendously positive relationship with him.

I'm the youngest of four children. My sisters are 10 and 13 years older than me, and my brother is three years older. After our father passed away, my oldest sister, who I'm very close with, asked me, "Who do you think was Dad's favorite?"

When she asked, my first thought was: What a ridiculous question.

My dad took me to the horse races every month. He nurtured my coin-collecting hobby, driving me all over the Washington, D.C. area to explore coin shops. He never missed a recital, musical, or school performance, and he always sat in the front row, standing, clapping, and cheering louder than anyone in the room when it ended.

Every night after dinner, he'd ask me to go for a walk. He loved throwing me the football as I ran routes up and down our neighborhood streets. On Sundays, he'd wake up at 6 a.m. to help me deliver my paper route. The newspapers were too heavy for me to carry while on my bike, so he'd insist on pushing a cart full of them while I walked each one up to my neighbors' doors.

So when my sister asked this question, I really thought she was just kidding. I told her it was *so* obvious that I was his favorite. Then she said something that sticks with me until today.

Every sibling felt the exact same way.

Mic drop moment.

Looking back, even though I thought I was emotionally constipated from the lack of sadness from his death, maybe it was because he did such a good job of raising me.

When my mother died, I cried for about a week, but after that, I didn't feel sad. I had been much closer to her since my father passed away, and I wasn't crying out of regret, or because I missed her cooking, or because I still needed her. I had already stepped into full independence, and I had helped take care of her in her final years. I cried simply because I missed her. Still, I felt a little guilty that the sadness didn't linger longer.

Is it possible that this is the mark of a strong relationship?

Maybe I was able to say goodbye without the weight of unresolved feelings, deep mourning, or guilt?

I've noticed something surprising over the years: children who had dysfunctional relationships with their parents often suffer more when that parent dies, not less.

You'd think it would be the opposite. That those with strained or painful relationships would feel relief, finally free from the burden of unresolved tension. And that those with healthy bonds would feel the greatest sense of loss.

It doesn't usually work that way. When a parent passes away and the relationship was never healed, it leaves behind a heavy weight of unfinished business. The healing words were never said and forgiveness was never offered. That's why if you blame your parents for your anxiety, low self-esteem, or emotional wounds, one of the greatest gifts you can give yourself is forgiveness before they're gone. Not for their sake, but for yours.

What's more likely is that a woman marries a man who didn't show signs of Emotional Constipation at first, but developed it over time—likely because he feels disrespected in the relationship.

For most men, respect is the deepest emotional need, even more than love. When a man feels respected, he opens up. He gives. He engages. But when that respect is missing, whether that feeling is legit or not, especially if he is constantly criticized, dismissed, or belittled, he often shuts down emotionally. The "store" that once offered connection, vulnerability, and affection is suddenly closed for business.

On the other hand, a woman's primary emotional need is usually love, not just in the romantic sense, but in feeling cherished, safe, and emotionally connected. That's how she feels validated. So when she doesn't feel loved, she may withdraw respect. And when he doesn't feel respected, he withholds love or emotional connection—creating a painful, self-reinforcing cycle.

If you feel your husband is emotionally closed off and isn't socially awkward, try finding something to respect him for. Treat a man with respect and he will *become* a man you respect.

"Honey, thank you so much for staying out of the kitchen while I make dinner."

"Thank you so much for leaving me space in the garage so I have room to get out of my car."

"I really appreciate you leaving your socks and underwear on the floor so I know that they need to go into the wash." (Sarcastically)

Women who struggle with emotional constipation are still generally more capable of expressing their feelings than most men. I'm not entirely sure where this outdated idea of "being a man" as someone who keeps everything bottled up came from. Who decided that masculinity means suppressing your emotions or refusing to be vulnerable—especially with someone you love?

Constipation of any kind is not healthy, but at least the physical kind will heal itself with some prunes, whereas the emotional kind will leave you feeling like you're living with a life sucking Emotional Vampire. However, you get to choose your spouse, boyfriend, or girlfriend, but you get no choice with this next category of Emotional Vampire.

Parents, Brothers, Sisters, Spouses, or In-laws

"There's no unsubscribe option for family."

If I had to guess the most common type of Emotional Vampire, this would be it. And unfortunately, they're often the people closest to us—family members, siblings, and even parents. These are the relationships that tend to drain us the most because we can't exactly cut them off, yet we can't always handle them either.

I'd be willing to bet that almost everyone reading this book has at least one of these people in their life. And if that's true, here's the uncomfortable flip side: that means most of us are probably Emotional Vampires in someone else's story too.

There's also a good chance you'd place these family members into multiple categories throughout this book. That's exactly why this deserves its own section. Here's the thing: if you weren't related to them, you'd probably have a lot more empathy. You might even find them quirky or endearing. But because you are family, the dynamic is different. You don't get to walk away. You have to show up, at holidays, birthdays, whether you feel like it or not.

Not all of your relatives are Emotional Vampires. It's just that the nature of the relationship makes everything feel more intense… and more draining.

You may be best friends with your mom if she was not your mom.

Case study: *Recently my two teenage daughters were fighting over a pair of shoes. I quickly informed them that if it happened to be one of their friends who wanted to borrow their shoes, they would gladly oblige. However, since they are sisters who are close in age, it became a point of contention. Once I mentioned this, they agreed and the argument was over with. (Yes, I admit I have children who get along very well and that is not always the case.)*

I believe this may be an issue in almost every family. These relationships are so close that you lose all ability to be empathetic with your sibling or parent.

Case study: *I was coaching a couple in Brooklyn about a year ago over lunch. They wanted to marry each other, but their parents dissuaded them from tying the knot. The issue was one of the parents had been in some sort of business deal with the other set of parents. They accused each other of fraud and are completely disgusted with the idea of their children getting married. We discussed the situation for about an hour.*

If you were giving them advice, how do you think you would advise them?

After some time talking to them and thinking it over, the deciding factor was their age. The man was 41 and the woman was 39, and they were both never married. I advised them to get married, and to move away from their parents who lived in the Long Island area. I told them if they were 20 and 21, I would probably not recommend it, but at their age, they are mature enough to handle the situation, but at a distance. Once children are in the picture, chances are the parents will calm down and will be able to form a more healthy relationship. Maybe they will not see each other's family every week, but one or two times a year. It is amazing how a new grandchild can help someone to heal much faster than years of therapy.

I regularly meet students who come from dysfunctional families. Some have divorced parents, others were raised by narcissists, or what they often describe vaguely as, "It's complicated." When I suggest that they consider creating physical or emotional distance, maybe even moving away, many of them look at me with guilt in their eyes. I tell them plainly: you have to protect your happiness.

If a relationship with a parent is causing emotional turmoil, then something has to change. That change might mean setting firm boundaries, limiting contact, or seeing them less often. You can still love someone and decide not to let them hurt you anymore.

There is a popular saying: "Hurt people hurt people." There is a lot of truth to this.

My mother and sister didn't have the best relationship, so when it came time for my sister to choose a college, my father gently encouraged her to leave town and study in South Florida. He used to travel there for business, and we had close relatives in the area, but more importantly, he understood that putting distance between his daughter and her mother was crucial for her emotional well-being.

And he was absolutely right.

My sister went on to build a very happy life for herself. She maintained a relationship with our mother, but it was defined by clear boundaries, ones that made the relationship sustainable and protected her inner peace. Sure, 'sustainable' doesn't mean it was warm and fuzzy, and it wasn't the kind of idealized mother-daughter relationship people often imagine. But sometimes, you have to take what's possible, not what's perfect. Honestly, in nine out of ten similar situations to this one, the mother and daughter wouldn't be speaking at all. I'll share more about this later.

How many people do you know who no longer speak to a parent or sibling? Sadly, it's more common than we like to admit.

In some cases, cutting ties is the only way someone can protect their emotional well-being. However, a limited relationship—even a small, distant one—is better than no relationship at all. If keeping the connection means creating strong boundaries and minimizing contact, that's okay. Sometimes, preserving your peace means redefining what "family" looks like.

Boundaries are essential for protecting our emotional well-being. In-laws, especially mother's-in-law, often struggle to recognize where those boundaries should lie when it comes to their children's marriages. And that brings us to our next category of Emotional Vampires...

Boundary Invaders

*"They treat your
'Do not disturb sign'
as a suggestion."*

Boundary invaders are people who see the relationship very differently than you do. That misalignment can show up in all kinds of ways—but one of the most common examples I see is in friendships between young men and women, particularly in their teens and twenties.

Here's what often happens: a young man and woman spend time together, hang out regularly, maybe talk every day, but they're "just friends." At least, that's how it's labeled. In many of these cases, especially from the guy's side, he's hoping it turns into something more. He may genuinely enjoy her company, but underneath the friendship is the quiet (or not-so-quiet) hope that it becomes romantic.

Now, I know I'll probably take some heat for saying this, but here it is: in most cases, men and women aren't "just friends." Not because it's impossible, but because there's often an unspoken dynamic coming from the men's side.

Men, in general, will want to sleep with the woman.

It creates a relationship imbalance and, over time, leads to confusion, hurt feelings, and crossed boundaries.

If a guy insists that he has zero romantic or physical interest in his close female friend, in many cases, he's probably not being entirely honest.

Now, this dynamic doesn't always work the same way in reverse. Women often enjoy male friendships because of the attention and validation they receive. It feels good to be valued, listened to, and admired. Plus, having a male friend can be a refreshing change of pace, especially for women who struggle to connect with other women. I've met many women who simply find male friendships easier—less drama and no constant comparison of each other.

Some guys may start off with similar intentions, but eventually, more often than not, the desire for something physical or romantic creeps in. It may not be spoken, but it's there, simmering beneath the surface.

Here's the challenge with men and women being "just friends"—physical touch, even something as simple as a hug or casual contact, can trigger the release of oxytocin. As discussed earlier in the chapter on narcissists, this so-called "love hormone" fuels sexual attraction and helps form romantic attachments. This sneaky chemical is great for bonding—but not so great for keeping things strictly platonic.

Oxytocin is both a hormone and a neurotransmitter, and it does both well. This is why if a man is friends with a woman he is *not* attracted to, which is probably rare, he may come to change his mind about them the more there is an increase in oxytocin production.

***Case study:** When I used to travel to conventions, I'd often see the same people year after year. One of the larger companies I did business with had a woman who handled all of their transactions. She was about ten years older than me and had what you might call a classic "biker chick" vibe—she smoked, was a bit rough around the edges, and very overweight.*

She was very sweet, though, and I interacted with her a lot because of how much business I did with her company. And every time we saw each other—probably eight times a year for nearly 30 years—she'd greet me with a hug.

Then one day, after one of those familiar hugs, I remember thinking to myself, "She's actually... not that bad."

That's when it hit me: This is how so many poor relationships begin.

Physical touch, even something as innocent as a hug, doesn't care about age gaps, crooked yellow teeth, or whether someone is your type. It just tricks your brain into forming a connection, whether you planned to or not.

Boundary Invaders can also show up as a new neighbor who just moved in. They may start name-dropping you as a "friend" to boost their own social standing, even though you barely know them or wouldn't consider the relationship that close.

It's not necessarily malicious, but it's presumptive when someone skips steps in the natural progression of connection.

Another type of boundary invader is someone who inserts themselves into conversations you consider private. They may not mean harm, but they ignore social cues, hovering nearby, chiming in uninvited, or acting like every conversation is open to the public. It's annoying and intrusive. It can make you feel like you have no personal space.

Have you ever had a conversation with a close talker? You know, the kind of person who thinks 6 inches is a perfectly acceptable conversation distance. The worst is when you can actually smell their breath—that's when my brain starts screaming, "Run away!"

Boundary Invaders bother us because they violate our sense of protected space. That's why setting boundaries isn't just a nice idea, but essential to emotional well-being.

Not every thought deserves a mic; not every person deserves access to your space; and not everyone deserves your emotional energy like they're eating "Endless Apps" at TGI Fridays. Boundaries are the fence you build around your peace and you're the only one who gets to decide who, or what comes through that gate. Unless, of course, you're not so sure you can trust your own decisions—in which case, you might be dealing with the next type of Emotional Vampire... the Second-Guessers!

The Second Guessers

*"I was feeling confident...
but luckily, you fixed that."*

Second guessers will occupy your time with self-doubt about their decisions and the decisions of others. They question everything they do and always wonder if they made the correct choice. One thing about second guessers, you will never confuse one with a narcissist. In fact, out of all the categories of Emotional Vampires, second guessers and narcissists will probably never overlap like many of the other categories.

Second guessers constantly seek reassurance for their decisions. Double and triple checking repeatedly. They can drain your energy because they may take forever when deciding what they need to wear just to go to the grocery store. This is probably more indicative of how a teenager acts, but it can just as easily be your 45 year old wife.

I am aware that I am insinuating that women are more concerned about how they dress in public, but unless a middle aged man is effeminate, men don't care nearly as much.

This is why a man needs to learn how to compliment his wife on her clothing. If not, she will keep buying clothing until he notices.

Even if a man does not care about fashion, or even likes his wife's clothes, giving her a positive comment will save him lots of money. A simple, "Wow, that looks great on you," can go a long way. Whether it's heartfelt or strategic, that one compliment might just save him hundreds of dollars… and a few hours at the mall.

Want to blow your wife's mind? Casually say, "Hey, remember that dress you wore to Sarah's wedding six months ago? You looked amazing in it." She'll freeze in her tracks and probably wonder if you've been replaced by an AI robot. That thoughtful comment sticks with her and it does more than just flatter. It boosts her confidence and reassures without second-guessing herself.

The company Stitch Fix was probably started by someone who recognized that choosing clothes is a big problem for second guessers. The company's website states that the business was formed:

"…to blend the human element of personal styling with high-quality clothing and proprietary algorithms."

That is a nice way of saying, "we started the company because shoppers are so wishy-washy that we took the guesswork out of buying clothes." The founder, Katrina Lake, figured out that second guessers will buy a lot more clothes if someone chooses the clothes for them. She shipped the first Stitch Fix order out of her Cambridge apartment in 2011 while attending Harvard, and today the company has brought the exclusive shopping experience to millions of men and women nationwide. This is just another indication about how many potential second guessers there are in the world.

Second guessers can also frustrate you at a restaurant. They can sit there and stare at the menu for 20 minutes like they're taking their SAT's and still have no idea what they want. Then when they do order, they will ask the waiter 14 questions, finally order the salmon... then switch to the chicken... then ask if it's too late to go back to the salmon. And once the food arrives? You guessed it—they should've ordered what *you* got. Second-Guessers can turn a simple dinner out into a full-blown emotional endurance test.

Here are some signs that someone might be a second guesser:

- They change their minds often, going back and forth on their choices.
- After making a choice, they dwell on whether it was the right one.
- They break down every possible outcome, sometimes to the point of paralysis.

- They avoid making decisions altogether or rely on others to decide for them.
- They question decisions made by others, even after agreeing initially.

Is it possible that your partner is a second-guesser, or you may be one yourself? If you happen to be married to one, just be thankful that they are not the next category of an Emotional Vampire.

The Projectors

*"It's Not Me,
It's Definitely You."*

When someone is projecting, they're unconsciously offloading their own feelings, thoughts, or insecurities onto you. Their inner self-doubt becomes your supposed flaw. What they accuse you of—being selfish, manipulative, jealous—is often exactly what they're guilty of themselves. In truth, they're not seeing you clearly at all; they're seeing a reflection of their own unresolved issues. Projection isn't about who you are—it's about what they can't face in themselves.

If it happens to be a romantic relationship, a co-worker, boss, or a family member, it can be a very challenging dilemma. You are probably thinking to yourselves, "What are they talking about? That is exactly what they are themselves!"

It can drain the emotional energy needed to keep a relationship healthy and it usually does not end up well. This is a dangerous Emotional Vampire because not only are they causing you stress and anxiety, they are living a lie. Lies are like Pringles—once you pop, you can't stop... and pretty soon the whole relationship is in the can.

Here are some signs to watch for if someone is projecting and blaming you for things they struggle with themselves:

- They accuse you of things that don't reflect who you are. For example, they might say, "You're so jealous," when in reality, they're the one showing jealousy.

- Their criticism feels unusually intense. Their reaction seems way out of proportion—like they're upset about something deeper than the situation at hand. Maybe you did or said something that hit a nerve.

- They refuse to take ownership. Instead of acknowledging their own flaws, they flip the script and make you the problem.

- You constantly feel the need to defend yourself against lies. You catch yourself thinking, "That's not even true. Why are they saying this about me?"

This has never been more obvious than in today's world. You turn on the news and feel like society is losing both its mind and its morals. What was once right is now called wrong, and what was clearly wrong is being celebrated. Reality feels twisted—and before you know it, you're wondering if you've somehow slipped into an alternate universe.

False Dichotomies

A False Dichotomy is a logical fallacy that presents only two options, outcomes, viewpoints, or sides when there are actually more—split into two extreme sides, with little room for nuance or middle ground.

"You're either with us or against us."

This ignores the possibility that someone could be neutral, supportive in some ways but critical in others. It is a problem because False Dichotomies oversimplify complex issues and can manipulate people into choosing one side by ignoring nuance or alternatives.

Other examples:

"We either ban all guns or have complete chaos."

"If you don't love me, you must hate me."

"You either succeed or you're a failure."

Another example of a False Dichotomy is when one romantic partner says to the other, "You always do this…". This is usually a form of overgeneralization and a frequent tactic in arguments. It implies that a partner is *always* a certain way—leaving no room for nuance.

Partner leaves dishes in the sink once and it leads to: "You always do this!"

Sometimes, "You always do this…" bursts out in the heat of the moment when someone is overwhelmed, not necessarily trying to be unfair, but reacting emotionally.

In reality, most situations are more complex and involve a spectrum of possibilities. Recognizing False Dichotomies helps promote clearer and more balanced thinking.

We see this play out in politics every day: one side believes their candidate is always right, while the other side can do no right at all. It's the classic black-and-white mindset—everything is either completely good or completely bad. But the real world doesn't work that way. Life comes in shades, and a lot of it is gray. That means people aren't entirely right or entirely wrong; sometimes they get it right, sometimes they miss the mark. Pretending otherwise only makes us more divided and less honest.

We just witnessed a classic example during both of Trump's elections and presidencies. You rarely hear a talking head both criticize and praise the President in the same breath. Either he's the worst president ever—or he's the best president ever. How is it possible that so many people hold such wildly divergent views of the same man?

Is it possible that some things he does are disgusting, while other things he does are moral and courageous?

Yes! It can be both.

Are we regressing into a tribal society—where loyalty to "our kind" trumps logic (no pun intended), reason, and even basic decency? Call it what you want: ideological extremism, cultural fragmentation, echo chambers, binary thinking, ideological bifurcation, or just another chapter in the ongoing culture war. No matter the label, the result is the same: a society that's moving backwards, not forwards.

I believe we've done this to ourselves—and as much as I hate to say it, a big part of it stems from capitalism. Now don't get me wrong—I love capitalism, but when profit becomes more important than principles, when success trumps ethics, society starts to pay the price.

I grew up near Potomac, Maryland—an extremely wealthy suburb of Washington, D.C. Back then, the local shopping center was full of charm: bookstores, ice cream shops, cozy mom-and-pop restaurants, and essential stops like grocery and drug stores. But as incomes rose, so did rents—eventually pricing out the smaller, family-run businesses. Today, if you live in that area and want a scoop of ice cream, you're driving 25 minutes. What replaced those shops? Banks. Lots of them. With so much cash flowing through the community, banks could easily afford the high rents that small businesses couldn't. Sure, they'll offer you a cup of coffee while you wait for your wire transfer—but don't expect a scoop of mint chocolate chip.

If money becomes the *sole* purpose of our lives, then our self-worth becomes our net worth—and suddenly, driving anything less than a brand-new BMW starts to feel like a personal failure. No wonder so many people have low self-esteem.

It wasn't just a shift in values—it was a shift in technology that ushered in all this noise. Not too long ago, the news was just... the news. You'd tune in at 7 p.m. and hear it from trusted voices like Walter Cronkite, Peter Jennings, Tom Brokaw, or even Barbara Walters. That was it—three channels, three anchors and mostly, with some nuances, one version of reality. No screaming panels or clickbait chaos. Just the facts—served once daily.

Then in 1980, Roone Arledge shook things up by launching a new program on ABC with Ted Koppel at the helm—a role he held until his retirement in 2005. Nightline was a game changer. Suddenly, news wasn't just something you got with your morning coffee or during dinner—it followed you to bed. At 11:30pm, just when you were winding down, the world wound back up, and you thought *that* was too much news?

Then came September 11, 2001. As the terrorist attacks unfolded in New York and Washington, something new appeared on our TV screens: the scrolling news ticker. At first, it felt like a temporary response to an unprecedented crisis just a way to keep up with the flood of information. But what many assumed was a short-term fix quickly became a permanent fixture. Though news tickers existed before 9/11, it was the urgency and scale of that day that cemented them into the DNA of 24-hour news.

During this time, many of us began shifting how we consumed news. We moved from traditional television—where networks couldn't track much beyond viewership ratings—to the internet, where every click, scroll, and share became valuable data. Suddenly, journalism wasn't just about informing the public—it became a way for news organizations to mine your preferences, predict your behavior, and shape the content you'd see next. News stopped simply reporting on what we thought—and started influencing it.

This technological shift began tracking your every reaction and how long you watched. Suddenly, what was meant to be an unbiased source of information turned into a high-powered money machine. The more outrage or confirmation bias they served, the more clicks they earned. News wasn't just reported—it was engineered. And as profits grew, so did the polarization: MSNBC leans left, Fox News leans right, and objectivity quietly left the building.

The business model of major media didn't just drift from mild bias—it took a hard turn into full-blown manipulation. What used to be news slowly morphed into narrative, tailored not to inform, but to influence.

When profits become the primary incentive, people will chase them—as long as it's legal. Scott Adams, in his book Loserthink, put it bluntly: "If something is legal and profitable, it will happen—a lot." He coined the term *political warming* to describe how the media manipulates public perception. Scott continued:

"The business model of the press manipulated our brains until our emotions overwhelmed whatever traces of rationality we started with…truth routinely loses out to emotion-based click-bait versions of reality."

Since the press is incentivized to spotlight the most sensational problems—and our brains are already wired with built-in bias—confirmation bias kicks in hard, reinforcing our belief that we're absolutely right… and everyone on the other side is clearly out of their minds.

We naturally gravitate toward news sources that tell us what we want to hear, not necessarily what we need to hear. This leads to a sensationalized media landscape, where emotion trumps accuracy. When given a choice between watching a baby take its first steps or a fiery car crash, our brains light up for the wreck every time. Why? Because our neurons crave the adrenaline of chaos—even if it's disturbing. And once we start feeding that craving, the algorithm happily delivers more of the same. It becomes a self-reinforcing loop, and before we know it, we're living inside an echo chamber of extremes. That's how false dichotomies are born.

False dichotomies are everywhere in our society. Consider hot-button topics like LGBTQ rights, vaccines, abortion, and immigration—where people are often pressured to choose one side completely against the other.

At many LGBTQ marches, you'll often see signs that say "Free Palestine"—a message aimed directly against the only Jewish state in the world. The irony? Israel happens to have some of the most progressive laws for LGBTQ rights anywhere in the Middle East. Tel Aviv even hosts the largest Pride parade in the Middle East—okay, maybe it's the *only* one in the Middle-east, but that's exactly my point!

Meanwhile, in many of the surrounding countries, including those often championed in these protests, being gay is not just taboo; it's illegal and, in many places, punishable by death. There are documented cases, including disturbing footage of individuals in Gaza being thrown off rooftops simply for being gay.

It's worth asking: why is Israel, one of the few places in the region where LGBTQ people can live openly and safely, while some in the LGBTQ community are supporting regimes with openly brutal policies that go directly against what they are marching for?

Is this a case of a False Dichotomy meeting a Projector?

Carl Jung was a Swiss psychiatrist and the founder of analytical psychology. He believed that scapegoating reveals something deep about how our minds work. According to Jung, every person has a hidden "shadow" side—parts of ourselves we don't want to admit. As he put it in Archetypes and the Collective Unconscious, "The shadow personifies everything that the subject refuses to acknowledge about himself."

These shadow parts often cause us discomfort, and we spend a lot of energy denying they exist. But the only way we recognize them is through projection—seeing in others what we can't face in ourselves.

On one hand, there's the False Dichotomy that you must be either completely pro-LGBTQ or entirely anti-LGBTQ—with no room for nuance or middle ground. On the other hand, there's Projection: publicly supporting openly brutal regimes that crush the very democratic values you claim to stand for—just because those regimes happen to align with your ideological stance.

These aren't just contradictions—they're betrayals of reason. The demand for blind allegiance and the defense of tyrants reveal less about justice and more about our own shadows: the fears, biases, and hypocrisies we'd rather not admit. Jung saw this clearly, and his insights strip away the excuses.

In short, we all have parts of ourselves that we're not proud of and sometimes deny exists: hate, lust, greed, selfishness, cruelty, jealousy, narcissism, laziness—you can probably think of some others. Some argue that the traits we dislike most in other people are the traits we (consciously or subconsciously) dislike most about ourselves. And sometimes we can become so adamant to deny that aspect of ourselves that we seek it out and furiously denounce those traits in other people.

If we are honest, we'll recognize that there are times we both personally and collectively don't live up to our own values or how we want to see ourselves.

As a general rule: if you want to understand someone's desires, pay attention to what they accuse others of—because more often than not, they're revealing what they secretly want themselves.

Projecting is a dangerous trait and it can lead to devastating results. Although the next Emotional Vampire is not *nearly* as destructive…unless you count your ex texting you 47 times a day with 'You don't love me anymore? Annoying? For sure! Dangerous? Only to your sanity.

The Overly Dependent

*"You're their emotional Airbnb…
always open for business
and trashed by checkout."*

Over dependence occurs when you can't fulfill your needs on your own, so you rely on someone else to fulfill them for you. This can be a friend, spouse, or relative. If you can't live without someone's emotional, or even physical support, that can suggest your relationship has veered toward an unhealthy level of dependence.

I understand there are instances when a couple is aging and one has to take care of the other. This is not the situation I am referring to here. I am referring to a healthy young person or a couple where one person is overly dependent on the other.

These are people who rely on you for constant emotional or physical support, to the point of becoming a burden.

They struggle to take initiative or solve problems on their own. This is why one of my goals for parenting is to raise independent, emotionally healthy children. I do not want my children to have to be reliant on someone else.

Someone with these issues probably has low self-esteem. They may not trust their own judgments or abilities. They may have a fear of failure or won't try anything without the help of someone else. This fear of failure can lead to procrastination.

They may tell themselves, "Why bother starting if it won't be perfect?" This mindset can operate quietly in the background, whether consciously or not. Many times, it stems from past experiences of harsh criticism that chipped away at their confidence. It's a powerful reminder for anyone in a relationship: excessive criticism doesn't build better behavior—it builds fear. It can shut down a person's desire to take risks or pursue anything meaningful. If we want the people we love to grow, we must become their encouragers, not their silencers.

I could've called this chapter The Procrastinators, but procrastinators don't usually drain your energy—unless you're married to one. They may not always be overly dependent on others, but those who are overly dependent are often world-class procrastinators.

Procrastination doesn't just delay dreams—it buries them. It can hold you back from launching that business, starting that fitness program, pursuing a degree, or stepping into a meaningful relationship. Maybe you've told yourself, "Why make the bed if it's just going to get messy again?" But that mindset keeps you stuck exactly where you are.

Here's the truth: you can't fail at something you never try. And while failure gets a bad rap, it's actually proof that you moved and you cared enough to show up. The real danger isn't falling short—it's never stepping forward.

Emotionally healthy people don't care about being perfect. It's about being willing to take the first step and not waiting for that perfect moment.

This is a common challenge in marriages where passion has started to fade. One spouse may begin to wish their partner didn't have a particular flaw or struggle, imagining that life would be easier with someone else. But what they often fail to realize is this: trading spouses doesn't eliminate problems—it simply swaps one set of challenges for another. The new partner may come with different issues, some of which may be even harder to live with. The illusion that happiness lies in someone new often ignores the reality that all relationships require patience and the willingness to love someone through their imperfections.

They may have also come from a background where everything was given to them and they never had to do anything for themselves. This is overindulging and can be just as bad as under indulging. This often stems from helicopter parenting—where parents hover, fix, and shield—believing they're helping, but ultimately preventing growth. They're left blinking like deer in the headlights of adulthood, wondering why the world doesn't come with a user manual and a snack.

Case study: *We host many guests from South Africa. Besides having the most amazing accents, they are the nicest people! The whites in South Africa have it pretty good—most of them are pretty wealthy. Since the cost of living is so low, most families have several housekeepers, landscapers and drivers. They are used to having everything done for them, including cooking, cleaning, and laundry.*

I will usually hint to my guests that if you have been to a meal with us 3 times, you have to help with clean-up. I do this to help take the burden off of my wife. Many times, my South Africans don't lift a finger. They are so used to being served hand and foot and overly dependent on help that the idea of helping your host clean-up is a foreign thought to them.

In my class, From Swipe Right to Wedding Night: Make Yourself Irresistibly Marriageable, one of the core principles I teach is simple: take responsibility. This is something that the Overly Dependent don't do very well.

Imagine this—you're at a dinner party, and a young man finishes his meal, stands up, and begins clearing everyone's plates… without being asked. If you're a single woman, don't tell me that doesn't make him at least 200% hotter on the spot.

It's the same feeling a wife gets watching her husband read The Very Hungry Caterpillar for the fifth time to their toddler—complete with voices. Now, I'm not a woman, but I'd wager that scene melts more hearts than a dozen roses and a candlelit dinner combined. Real responsibility is attractive. It's not about grand gestures—it's about showing up and being the kind of person who makes life easier, not heavier.

Imagine a hardworking Midwestern man marrying someone who's never had to lift a finger in her life. If that mindset carries into the marriage, he'll likely struggle to respect her. The same is true in reverse. When a husband lounges around all day while his wife handles the cooking, shopping, and raising the children, her respect for him will inevitably fade. When one partner becomes overly dependent on the other, the relationship starts to shift from a friend and lover to something that feels more like a staff member.

I've coached many married couples whose relationship hit turbulence—and in many instances, the root cause was one spouse working for the other.

Consider the classic example which you have probably experienced: a dentist who hires his wife as his office assistant, or in my field, a husband who brings his wife in to help with invoices and admin work. I've asked my wife to step in during times when I was overwhelmed, but I made sure to keep it occasional. Why? Because when one partner takes on a role in the other's business, it can quietly shift the relationship. It's surprisingly easy in that situation to become overly dependent on your spouse for your work.

On paper, it makes sense—it's convenient, cost-effective, and there's already trust. However, in reality, the dynamic often shifts from husband/wife to boss/employee. Then the bedroom turns into a boardroom and suddenly you're not pillow-talking, you're power-pointing. The only thing getting laid off here is romance.

When one spouse becomes professionally over-dependent on the other, it can blur emotional roles and chip away at the romance that made the relationship work in the first place. When work starts taking priority over love, it's time to reassess the arrangement.

Being overly dependent may be from a past trauma that has not allowed you to go out on your own because of fear of going back to that same place.

Case study: I once had a girlfriend who appeared on the surface to be very confident. Unfortunately, when the relationship started to falter a bit, she started calling me every 2 minutes. I wish I was exaggerating. I ended up driving to the beach with my friends and turned my phone off for a few days. I felt like I was being strangled. That is not what a healthy relationship looks like. Obviously, that was the end of that.

I realize that people may marry someone who either comes from the same background, has the same emotional flaw, or has a familiar past. We're drawn to what feels familiar—even if it's dysfunctional. People feel comfortable with familiarity, this is why women tend to marry people that resemble their father and men tend to marry people that resemble their mother. Then there are the people that marry people that look like themselves! If what you have in common is an unresolved emotional weakness, the marriage can struggle deeply. And sometimes, it's only much later that you realize… you didn't just marry a person—you married your own flaw in disguise.

Case study: *We knew a couple who both are great! Unfortunately, they were separated for a while which was a shock for us. The wife admitted to us that when she was dating, she passed on perfectly good men. It was not until she met her current husband that she felt like marrying him. She felt comfortable with him because she saw that they were both carrying emotional burdens. Thankfully they worked this out and are back together.*

Put an end to being overly dependent, and you'll find yourself being a much happier person not having to rely on others for your emotional or physical needs. However, what may be worse than being overly dependent is having to depend on someone to listen to your non-stop banter.

Non-Stop Talkers

"The Human Podcast That Won't Pause."

When I was in my early 20s, I went on a date with a very pretty young woman. Within minutes, I realized she could not stop talking. I genuinely started looking around for hidden cameras. I thought, this has to be a prank. I must be on Candid Camera. No one can talk this much without coming up for air. It was a herculean effort for me to just try to get in a few words. She was sweet, no doubt about it, but there was absolutely no way I could survive a second date. Thankfully, she met a guy and eventually got married…poor guy.

I hope he owns a good pair of noise-canceling headphones.

Although that date was a one and done, it was another lesson that I need to be aware of my own tendency to talk too much and take over a conversation, without having any regard for the person in front of me. Singles who are dating need to have the social savviness to recognize that consistent non-stop talking can drain their emotional energy. It is possible that people do this when they are nervous.

Do people realize they're completely sucking the air out of the room when they talk non-stop?

Sometimes, this habit stems from growing up in a large family—where getting a word in edgewise was a full-contact sport. Now, finally out of the chaos, they seize every opportunity to talk... and talk... and talk. Maybe they're just trying to make up for all those years of being talked over at the dinner table.

Or it could be the exact opposite, someone who was an only child. With no siblings to chat with, they spent years talking to their stuffed animals and waiting for someone to listen. Now that they've found a live audience, they're making up for a decade of silence.

Here are some other reasons why people talk so much and make it hard for you to get a word in edgewise:

1. They have no awareness that they talk too much.
2. They think the world revolves around them and they don't want to listen to anyone else. (Narcissistic tendencies)
3. They have a hearing issue so they would rather talk than listen.
4. They are compensating for being ignored earlier in their life.

5. They think they are the only ones with important information to share.
6. They are highly opinionated and don't have any respect for someone else's opinion.

Case study: *I was once at a town hall event for county officials who were running for office in an upcoming election. After the candidates spoke, the organizers set up a microphone in front of the stage to allow questions from the audience members. This will sometimes attract people who have never had the chance to voice their opinions in front of a large group of people. Invariably, instead of asking a question, they ramble on for 10 minutes with a story about something that happened and their opinion of how politicians should be handling the situation. A good moderator will anticipate this and ask the speaker to get right to the question.*

This is a case when someone has the chance to have their voice heard and they take advantage of it by dragging out their question.

I often run into the same issue when coaching a student— whether a dating question or self-esteem struggles. They'll launch into a long, winding story that can really drain me. So after a few minutes, I'll gently ask: Do you have a problem you want me to solve or a question you want me to answer? I know it might sound blunt, but when someone truly needs help, the fastest way to get there is by identifying the core issue. The backstory can often wait—and in many cases, it only clouds the situation. Too much information can muddy the waters and prevent any real solution from taking shape.

One of the best ways to avoid draining someone's emotional energy—especially in conversation—is to be clear and direct. This isn't just about romantic relationships; it applies to every kind of communication.

People have limited time, limited patience, and even more limited attention spans. If you ramble or circle the point too long, your message risks getting lost. But if you cut to the chase, people are far more likely to stay engaged and actually respond.

Respect their time. Respect your message. Be brief, be clear, and be heard.

This applies to emails too—sometimes, a single well-crafted sentence says more than a paragraph ever could. Clear, concise communication isn't just efficient; it leaves less room for confusion and misinterpretation.

Case Study: In some religious communities, couples who are dating often set clear phone boundaries early on—typically limiting calls to twice a week, no longer than 60 minutes each. Why? Because it spares both people from feeling obligated to stay on the phone when they're tired, busy, or just not in the mood. It also eliminates the awkward overthinking that happens when someone cuts a call short. Let's face it—phone chemistry is not real-life chemistry.

Have you ever had a phone relationship that felt electric… only to meet in person and feel… nothing? I can't be the only one. Teenagers—especially girls—are phone conversation pros. It's off the phone, in real life, where teenagers somehow manage to drain every ounce of emotional energy from a parent.

Teenagers: Where Logic Doesn't Exist

"Normal rules don't apply here"

This chapter wasn't even supposed to exist. I thought I had covered every category of Emotional Vampire—until one of my classes proved me wrong. A middle-aged couple came over, looking exhausted, and said, "Our teenager's a narcissist. She thinks the world owes her everything."

I felt for them—they weren't just venting, they were drowning. So I sat down with them and shared my advice.

A child psychologist once told me that dealing with teenagers is basically like living with someone who's temporarily brain-damaged. And the condition doesn't clear up until around age 25. Think of it as a long warranty period where the brain is still "under construction."

So what's a parent's mission? Simple: keep them close, keep them engaged, and keep them (at least somewhat) happy. Your job isn't to win every battle—it's to make sure they still like you enough to come back once their brain finishes downloading the adult software.

If your teen trusts you—if they know you've always got their back—they will eventually circle back and listen. But parents who rely on constant criticism, punishment, and yelling risk breaking that trust. And once it's gone, the damage can last decades.

I know this might sting to hear, but yelling doesn't make you an awesome parent—it makes you a louder one. And louder isn't better, especially with teenagers. Yelling is really just our frustration spilling out because we hate admitting we can't control everything, especially our children.

The good news? You can train yourself out of it. Some parents count to ten, others bite their tongue, and a few take it out on an innocent pillow in the next room. Whatever works. Once you realize yelling almost never gets you anywhere (other than maybe a sore throat), you'll stop wasting your energy on it.

For example, in our house, we have a simple rule: no mindless eating. Eating while distracted—especially in front of screens—can lead to unhealthy habits and weight gain. Most of my children follow this, but my oldest sometimes breaks the rule, munching while playing online chess like he's a grandmaster.

It's not a rule I enforce strictly, but he knows about it, and I remind him only occasionally—not to nag, but to show that I haven't forgotten. The most important part? I never eat while watching screens myself. At the very least, I don't want to be a hypocrite.

I believe that, eventually, he'll follow my example—becoming more mindful of his eating habits and leaving the multitasking for the chessboard, not his plate. Children will do what parents do, not what they say. If your teenagers continue to do something you don't want them to do, at a minimum, make sure you don't do it yourself—and one day they will listen to you.

Here's another key to understanding teenagers: whatever you forbid instantly becomes irresistible. Not everyone will agree with our approach, but we allow our kids to occasionally have wine at the dinner table, especially Friday nights when we drink it. They know it's available at home—but they also know the dangers of overdoing it. If I were to ban it completely, suddenly alcohol would transform from "meh" to the ultimate forbidden treasure.

If you keep your teenager happy and engaged, they'll want to stay involved in your life once their brain finally starts to mature. The parents who struggle later on are usually the ones who couldn't manage their anger, couldn't handle a little disrespect, or couldn't resist constant criticism. Those patterns drive a wedge that can last well beyond the teenage years.

Learn to let them down gently—slowly and thoughtfully. Instead of a flat-out "no," try phrases like:

"I don't think that would be a good idea."

"Let me think about it."

"I'll need to discuss it with your father first."

You can also offer alternatives you're comfortable with. For example:

"If you want to go bowling tonight, I'll take you. If you want to go without me, you'll need to wait until daytime."

This approach helps your teenager feel heard and respected, while still setting clear boundaries.

Is the advice I'm giving you foolproof? Honestly, probably not. But I've survived moving to another country with young teenagers, which is basically like trying to herd caffeinated cats through customs. My one goal: keep them happy. Make sure they have friends—even if those friends were not our favorites. As long as they're smiling now, there's a good chance that someday they'll look back and think, "Hey, maybe my parents weren't completely insane after all."

One more piece of parenting advice for teenagers: school isn't everything. What really matters for their future success is that they feel understood and supported by you. Who cares if they fail math? As long as they have friends and are happy, that's already a big win.

School isn't for everyone, and failing a class doesn't mean failing at life. Education is important, of course, but there are countless ways to learn and grow these days—many of which don't involve traditional classrooms.

It was actually my children who pushed me to teach a class on parenting. I got the inspiration during a school visit with my daughter—when we went to meet the principal for her interview. After just two minutes he said, "Your daughter is a superstar." That moment sparked the idea for the class title: "Raising Superstars." Maybe someday you'll be able to catch it on my YouTube channel.

The key is simple: keep your kids connected to you. Pray that someday they not only want a relationship with you, but also actually listen to you—and maybe even value your wisdom.

There's another category of Emotional Vampires—and every one of them is two years old. They can't pronounce half the alphabet, but they've got a PhD in emotional manipulation. One minute they're hugging your leg, the next they're melting down because you dared to peel their string cheese.

The Terrible Twos

"Tiny Dictators with Sippy Cups."

There's so much we can learn from dealing with young children that applies to every area of life. Parenting at this stage might be the hardest—at least until they become teenagers… then all bets are off, and you're basically negotiating with a sleep-deprived, hormone-fueled lawyer who thinks they know everything.

When a baby or toddler cries, they're usually soothed with a bottle, a snack, a cuddle, or a gentle rock to sleep. Up until around 18 months, they don't have much independent thought—they're simply reacting to the world around them. But somewhere between age 2 and 2.5, a major shift happens: they realize they have zero control over their own lives. Up to that point, every decision—what they eat, who they play with, when they sleep—is made by someone else. Then suddenly, they discover they have a will of their own. And that is when the terrible twos show up like an uninvited guest—certain they should be in charge.

Adults experience this same frustration too—just in grown-up packaging. Maybe they're stuck in a job they can't stand, but quitting isn't an option because that paycheck pays the bills. Or picture this: after a long, exhausting flight, the plane lands early (yay!)—only to sit on the tarmac for 45 minutes because there's no gate available (boo!). These moments tap into the same helpless feeling toddlers have: the realization that no matter how loud you scream, you're not in control.

The worst kind of powerlessness? Being stuck in a toxic marriage you can't escape—for any number of painful reasons. Just like a toddler, you may feel completely out of control. But here's the difference: adults are expected to manage their frustration. Sure, some cope with anger with late-night snacks, or less healthy habits like alcohol or drugs. But rarely does an adult throw themselves on the floor of a shopping mall, screaming at full volume.

You've probably seen that toddler-level meltdown in action: a small child flailing in the middle of a store, totally overwhelmed by life's injustices—the stuff of parental nightmares. Adults may not scream in the aisles, but the emotional chaos underneath can be just as loud.

That tantrum? It's not just about a broken cookie or the wrong color cup. It stems from a toddler's sudden realization that they have zero control over their lives. Ironically, it's not so different from what adults feel in certain situations—stuck in a job they hate, trapped in a toxic relationship, or circling the airport with no gate in sight. The difference is, grown-ups don't usually kick and scream on the floor.

One way to handle this is by letting them think they're in charge. Now, this trick doesn't always work, but it's a powerful tool to keep in your toolbox. When a child starts melting down, try offering a choice. Instead of always saying "no", which can quickly turn into background noise for them, let them feel like they're part of the decision. Give them two options that are both fine with you, "Do you want to wear the red shirt or the blue one?" Suddenly, they're not screaming because they've been empowered. You're not giving up control, you're just cleverly disguising it as freedom.

__Case study:__ My 3-year-old once went full meltdown mode over a pair of pajamas—as if I had handed her a burlap sack instead of her favorite clown pair. So, I calmly took those pajamas away and grabbed two completely different pairs from the drawer. Then I held them up and said, "Which of these would you like to wear?"

Instant shift.

Her brain went from "rage against the man" to "big man on campus." She picked one, put it on like a boss, and just like that... tantrum over.

When your toddler in the high chair reaches for a dinner knife on the table, your instinct might be to just snatch it away—and sometimes you have to, especially if it's a sharp one. But when it's safe to slow down a second, there's a smarter move: offer a distraction with a choice. Instead of simply saying "No," try offering a choice: "Would you rather play with your stuffed doggie or these jingly toy keys?"

Most of the time, they'll drop the knife and happily grab one of the other options because now they feel like they're in control. You redirected his attention without a power struggle.

If you've got a picky eater on your hands, one simple trick is to give them a choice: "Would you like broccoli or carrots tonight?" Giving them some say makes them feel in control and less likely to turn the dinner table into a battleground.

But if you really want to level up your veggie game, try turning their meal into a monster face. Use a plain fried egg as the base for the face, then decorate with veggies: a slice of red pepper for a mouth, cucumber rounds for eyes, carrot coins as ears, and shredded lettuce for the hair. Before you know it, they're giggling, nibbling, and asking you to make another monster—and suddenly, you're the Picasso of picky eating.

Another fun idea: turn snack time into track time with a veggie train! Start with a small toy engine at the front, then line up halved bell peppers as colorful train cars. Fill each one with cargo—carrot sticks, celery, cucumber slices, cherry tomatoes, or whatever veggies your child prefers. You can even "link" the cars together using thin veggie strips like zucchini ribbons or green beans for added flair. Then turn one of the pepper cars into a dipping station with something like Thousand Island dressing or hummus. Suddenly, munching on vegetables becomes fun. The longer the train, the more exciting it looks—and the more veggies your little conductor is likely to gobble up!

This idea of making healthy food fun ties perfectly into some of my core beliefs about marriage and self-esteem. If you turn love into a game you actually enjoy playing, you'll end up with more love in your life. And if you find ways to make the boring parts of life playful, you won't just enjoy life more—you'll build stronger self-esteem along the way. A little fun goes a long way, whether it's with broccoli or your beloved.

Unlike your friends—who you can choose to keep or ditch—you don't get to pick your kids. And yet, even though you didn't handpick them, you probably love them unconditionally, no matter how wild they act. But your spouse? The one you did choose? You might find yourself falling out of love or even filing for divorce. It doesn't seem to add up. What's the difference?

With your kids, you focus on their potential and their good qualities. With your spouse, you may fixate on their flaws—and that frustration can sometimes feel even worse than dealing with a toddler in full meltdown mode.

So here's the shift that if you get nothing else out of this book then this, it was well worth it: start focusing on why you fell in love with your partner in the first place. Revisit the traits that drew you in. Look through those original love goggles, and chances are, you'll start seeing them—and your relationship—very differently.

Boom.

Are You an Emotional Vampire?

"Be the light without the bite."

Ask a room full of people, "Who here is an Emotional Vampire?"

Crickets. Not a single hand goes up. Everyone suddenly becomes a beacon of emotional stability and good feeling vibes. But somehow, everyone has at least one Emotional Vampire in their life—someone who drains your energy like it's their full-time job. So how does that math work? Who's lying?

The truth is simple: we judge others by their behavior, but we judge ourselves by our intentions. This means that when other people do something wrong or upsetting, we tend to focus on their actions, but when we do something wrong, we often excuse ourselves based on why we did it.

For example, if someone is late, we might think they're careless or disrespectful. However, if we are late, we might think, "Well, I had a good reason—I hit traffic."

This is pointing out a common double standard in how we judge behavior—harsher on others, more forgiving toward ourselves. You ghost someone for three weeks? "I was just overwhelmed."

Someone does that to you? "They're toxic and emotionally unavailable."

Here's the kicker: If you can't spot the Emotional Vampire in your circle… it might be you.

It's not easy to look yourself in the mirror and admit the truth: you have flaws that are invisible to you—but crystal clear to everyone around you. Self-awareness isn't just about what you know—it's about being open to what you don't.

Because denial doesn't make you flawless. It just makes you the last to know.

Face the mirror, or stay blind. It's your choice.

Mike Zani, CEO of Predictive Index, offers a great way to think about self-awareness in his book The Science of Dream Teams. He introduces an analogy he learned from his time at his former consulting company.

Picture yourself wearing a shirt with writing on both the front and the back. On the front are all the compliments, strengths, and qualities you're proud of—the things you know about yourself and the world confirms. They're visible and easy to own. But then there's the back of the shirt. You can't see it, but everyone else can. That's where your blind spots live—the habits, flaws, or patterns you're unaware of, but others experience clearly.

And here's the catch: What's on the back matters just as much as what's on the front. Ignoring it doesn't make it disappear. It just makes you the only one not reading the whole story.

Self-awareness, then, is not just about knowing your strengths—it's about discovering and working on your weaknesses as well. This honesty lays the groundwork for a more authentic view of yourself and all your faults.

To become more self-aware, it's essential to invite the people around us to help identify what's on the "back of our shirts." This candid feedback can illuminate aspects of ourselves we may not even realize that are causing difficulties in our lives.

If you don't take to heart what's on the back of your shirt, you may repeat the same mistakes over and over and not even realize there is a problem. Here are two effective ways to discover what areas may be causing you to be an Emotional Vampire:

Seek out feedback and critique. Don't surround yourself solely with people who tell you what you want to hear. Seek out people willing to tell you what you *need* to hear—people who will call out what's on the back of your shirt. It is always nice to have people who are your "yes men." These are usually your friends who are always on your side and will give you positive feedback about all your decisions in your life. You don't want cheerleaders helping you to make decisions. And while that feels good, it's not what helps you grow. You need people who will tell you the truth without any bias involved.

I went through this problem while trying to improve the writing of my books. Almost everyone who read one of them would tell me they liked them. Even though their views were appreciated, those were all biased opinions. Unless my writing is very poor (which it probably isn't, since you've read this far), they'd probably like my books—because they like me. I want someone to show me the awkward sentence, the chapter that drags, the point that didn't land. I want to know everything that I can improve upon and all the mistakes that I don't know about. I don't want compliments. I want clarity. I want someone to tell me what is on the back of my shirt.

Don't fear criticism. Fear being the only one in the room who thinks their shirt is clean.

Accept Feedback Without Being Defensive. The next time someone gives you honest feedback, even if it is uncomfortable, just listen and thank them in the moment before taking the time to contemplate. Even if you don't agree with what they say, you have been given the gift of actually knowing how they feel. If you respond negatively or defensively, it will be the last time you get that honest feedback; no one will tell you again what's on the back of your shirt directly, they will just talk about it when you aren't around. Our first reaction to getting negative feedback is generally to give an excuse or rationalization of why their viewpoint is wrong. After some contemplation, your perspective may shift—and you might even find yourself agreeing with the criticism.

The hardest feedback is often the most valuable. Accept it with grace, and you'll only grow stronger.

***Case study:** I had just wrapped up teaching a dating class, and the vibe afterward was pretty calm—people hanging around, nibbling on desserts, waiting their turn to chat with me to get free dating advice.*

A few women decided to save time and approach me as a group. One of them, very direct, asked: "Why don't men ever ask me out for a second date? Am I doing something wrong?"

Now usually, this is where I'd gently dodge and say, "Who knows? Men are mysterious creatures." But this time... I actually did know.

And I was dreading saying it out loud.

During my talk, I noticed this woman. She had a look on her face like I'd just insulted her cat and grandmother in the same sentence. Total scowl. Some call it RBF. I made a mental note: She's definitely having a tough time in the dating world.

So when she asked, I took a breath and decided to tell her the truth—kindly, but directly. I said, "You're actually very cute when you smile. Like, really cute. But your resting face? It's telling a completely different story."

She looked shocked, like I told her that she had an upside down unibrow.

I tried to soften it with humor, saying, "You ever seen that Seinfeld episode where Jerry's date looked gorgeous in one light and like a goblin in another? Yeah... it's kind of like that. You're the gorgeous part—just make sure to leave the lights on."

She didn't love that. Okay, I really didn't tell her to leave the lights on, but I wanted to.

Here's the thing: don't ask the question if you don't want the truth. I didn't want to say it. Telling someone they're unknowingly scaring off dates with their face is not exactly a great way to make friends, but I genuinely felt like it was something she needed to hear.

I've told people hard truths before. I've had to tell single people that being significantly overweight is making their dating pool much, much smaller. Not because I enjoy playing the villain—but because I care. It's not fair, but it's real: people often judge skin-deep before they dig soul-deep.

And that's why I don't call myself a matchmaker. I call myself a mate maker. I don't just pair people up—I help them become someone others want to marry.

Hard truths. Soft delivery. Occasional jokes. And maybe... a little luck with some divine help.

I hope this young lady will eventually internalize this new awareness and be cognizant about smiling more when she is dating.

This case study isn't about someone who drains others emotionally—unless staring at a scowl face makes you exhausted, but it does shine a light on something just as challenging: facing our own flaws. The truth is, admitting we've got an issue isn't easy. It usually takes time—days, weeks, sometimes months—before we can look ourselves in the mirror and say, "Yeah… this is mine." And only then does the real work of change begin. Flip the mirror and you'll discover that self-awareness is like a superpower.

Taking ownership of your faults is the only way to start the process of healing. You actually have to say it to yourself out loud every day. Then your words will create your reality, then you will then be motivated to make the changes you need to be an emotional healer, not an Emotional Vampire.

Questions to ask yourself to determine if you are an Emotional Vampire:

- Do you have a hard time keeping friends for a long time?
- Do you have trouble getting 2nd or 3rd dates?
- Do you find that people will sometimes stop listening to you when you are talking with them?
- Are you upset when you are not the center of attention?
- Do you rationalize when what you consider a close friend suddenly ignores you?
- Do you have a hard time saying I am sorry, I was wrong, or I forgive you?

- Do you dominate conversations or interrupt others frequently?
- Do you often redirect conversations back to yourself?
- Do you need constant reassurance, compliments, or validation?

If 1 person calls you a donkey, don't believe them. If a 2nd person calls you a donkey, don't believe them. If a 3rd person calls you a donkey, buy a saddle. It takes deep introspection and breaking down of walls for the truth to seep in. If a person doesn't internalize that they have a serious flaw, they may do one of following 3 things:

Blame-They may accuse someone else for whatever it is you are accusing them of.

Argue-They want to bicker and fight with you about it.

Denial-They will not admit they are an Emotional Vampire.

These are all ***BAD*** reactions after you have informed someone that they drain you of your emotional energy. Don't sweat! It's possible that they probably shouldn't be in your life anyway. We will now do a friendship audit to determine whether someone really needs to be in your life. If we discover that they really do, then we will eventually learn how to make that relationship healthy.

As Andy Dufresne said in The Shawshank Redemption, "Get busy living or get busy dying." If you don't gain clarity about your own weaknesses and take steps to grow, relationship struggles will follow you throughout your life. That means doing the inner work—or else you'll be the friend that gets audited.

The Friendship Audit

*"Some friendships age
like wine—others like milk."*

Do you have many friends? Have you ever taken a moment to really consider what a friend truly is? It's possible that many of the people we call friends are in our lives more because of circumstance—present not because of intentional closeness, but simply because life placed them there.

For many, having friends provides a sense of identity and belonging. It makes us feel valued, seen, and accepted. But as we grow older, we often realize that some of these relationships are more like acquaintances. What we assumed were friends turn out to be connections tied to a particular circumstance or event.

This doesn't make those relationships meaningless—it just highlights how rare and valuable true friendship really is.

Just be aware that because you were friends in 4th grade does not mean you have to make them a friend for life. A true friend isn't just someone you've known for a long time—it's someone who grows with you, supports you, and shows up when it counts.

Most of your friends come from mainly the following:

- They attended your school
- They were in your class
- They are from your neighborhood
- They are parents of your children's friends
- They work in the same industry
- They play the same sports
- They attend the same church or synagogue
- They are facing similar emotional challenges
- They are an old friend from childhood

It's healthy to periodically audit your social circle and ask yourself: Does this person still add value to my life? Maybe what I call a friend may really just be an acquaintance.

Single people often gravitate toward other singles—they're in the same stage of life and usually share similar goals, whether it's seeking a relationship or just having fun. But once someone in that circle finds a romantic partner, they often drift away from their single friends. This reveals that what we called a 'friend' may have really just been a companion of circumstance.

Sometimes, letting go of a friendship can actually create space for more peace, growth, and authentic connection with the people that are your true friends.

Just like a financial audit reviews an individual's or organization's accounts, a friendship audit helps you examine who's adding value to your life, and who might be draining it. In this case, your most important asset isn't money, it's your emotional well-being.

If someone doesn't drain your emotional energy, meaning you genuinely enjoy being around them, they're easygoing, and rarely complain, then you may not need to audit that relationship. And if that describes most of your friendships, then one of two things is likely true:

You've already been intentional about who you allow into your inner circle. That shows wisdom and maturity.

You haven't yet realized that some of your friends are Emotional Vampires. Trust me—there's a good chance at least a few of them are—you just haven't realized it yet.

The main reason to conduct a friendship audit is to help improve your emotional health. If someone constantly drains your energy, it's important to ask yourself: Are they a vital part of my life? If the answer is yes, then the goal becomes finding ways to make that relationship healthier. If not, it may be time to start creating distance—or even phasing them out entirely.

How do you know if someone is truly essential? Here are a few examples of relationships that may be considered vital:

- Close family members, such as siblings and parents. (Note: While this book will briefly touch on spouses, that's a unique relationship that requires a different level of patience and nurturing.)
- Co-workers or supervisors you're required to work closely with
- Clients who generate significant revenue or high commissions
- Major donors to your organization
- Teammates in a competitive sports setting

Many of your relationships may not be optional, but how you manage them is within your control.

If someone isn't a vital part of your life, it's worth asking some honest questions to determine whether the relationship still deserves your valuable time:

- If you no longer shared the same interests, would you still be friends?
- Do you genuinely look forward to spending time with them?
- Do you feel drained or need to "recover" after hanging out?
- Do you hesitate to respond to their messages?
- Is it hard to stay focused or engaged during conversations with them?
- Are you drawn to them because you like to be drama adjacent and it adds excitement to your life?

- Are you holding onto the friendship simply because it's tied to nostalgic memories from childhood?

These questions aren't meant to shame—they're meant to bring clarity. Some friendships are only meant for one season, while others are meant to grow and evolve with you. The key is learning to tell the difference. There's no rule that says a past friendship must last forever, unless that's your personal rule. And even then, there's no rule that says you can't change your rules. Unless, of course, your rule is that you can't change your rules, in which case, you might just be a little stubborn.

The real question to ask yourself is: Is the price of admission worth it?

Is the emotional cost of this friendship too high?

Younger people are often more willing to maintain friendships that older individuals might walk away from—not just because older people have more knowledge, but because they've gained wisdom. They've learned, often through experience, that peace of mind is more valuable than forced connection.

Case study: *A friend once shared a struggle he had with someone on a non-profit board he served with. He described a man who dominated meetings with long, drawn-out, and often meandering commentary.*

According to him, this man would drain the room with his input.

Despite that, the man is a major donor to many organizations and is treated like an influential person wherever he goes. My friend suspected he might be on the spectrum, possibly with traits of Asperger's. He remarked that if this man weren't such a generous donor, most people wouldn't give him the time of day—let alone sit through his endless monologues.

This is one of those cases where people willingly tolerate being drained by his presence, simply for the reward of accessing his financial support.

You are the only one that can decide which friends are worth keeping and which ones you need to leave by the side of the road, not literally. Before we discuss how to make healthy relationships with people you can't ditch, we need to learn what it means to be a real friend.

What True Friendship Really Is

"Real friends bring snacks, not drama"

Back in ancient times, friendships weren't built on shared hobbies, like being a New York Jets fan—they were built on survival. It was basically, "You watch my back, I'll watch yours, and maybe we won't get eaten today." The bigger the tribe, the better the odds of fending off wild animals, rival clans, or that one guy who always showed up uninvited and set things on fire.

Women, understandably, wanted protection, which is why getting married young was less about romance and more about recruiting a personal bodyguard. Fast forward to today, and that instinct hasn't totally vanished. Why do women swoon over guys who can bench press a U-Haul truck? Because deep down, part of them is thinking, "If a bear bursts through the coffee shop window, at least my boyfriend can throw a table at it with one hand while still holding his latte in the other."

There are 2 stories from Jewish folklore written long ago about friendship that are a good barometer of what it really means to be a true friend.

During the time of the Roman Empire, two boys grew up together in the Babylonian Empire.[2] From a young age, they were inseparable—more like brothers than friends. As they grew older, life led them down different paths. One settled in a region under Roman control; the other in Syria, under a different rule. Despite the distance, their friendship never wavered.

Years later, the Roman friend traveled to Syria to visit his childhood companion. But during his stay, he was falsely accused of being a Roman spy. Without a fair trial, he was arrested and brought before the Syrian Emperor. The verdict was swift: death.

As he was being led away to await execution, the guards asked if he had any final wishes.

"Just one," he said. "Let me return to Rome to settle my affairs and say farewell to my family. I give you my word—I will return to face my sentence."

The Emperor laughed. "Do you take me for a fool? What guarantee do I have that you'll come back?"

The man answered, "I have a friend here in Syria. He'll stay in my place. If I fail to return, you can execute him instead."

---

2 From Shtei Yados (Two Hands). Kabbalah by Rabbi Menachem di Lonzano

This bold offer stunned the Emperor. "You'd risk your friend's life on your word alone?" he said. "And he'd agree to that?"

"Call him," the man replied. "He'll come."

Sure enough, the Syrian friend was summoned. Without hesitation, he agreed to take his friend's place in prison— and his life, if necessary.

The Emperor, both skeptical and intrigued, said, "Fine. You have 60 days. If you're not back by sunrise on the 60th day, your friend dies in your place."

The Roman returned home and began the painful task of putting his affairs in order. He wept with his family, said his goodbyes, and left with enough time to return. But fate intervened. The wind for the sailing galleys stalled for days, and no ships could leave the harbor. Helplessly delayed, he arrived in Syria at dawn—on the 60th day.

As the sun rose, the Syrian friend was already being led to his execution. A crowd had gathered—executions were public spectacles. Just as the sword was being drawn, the Roman burst through the crowd, shouting, "Stop! I've returned! Don't harm him!"

But the Syrian friend shook his head. "He's too late. The agreement stands. I took his place, and I will face the punishment."

"No," the Roman friend cried. "I'm here now. I made the promise. Let me die instead."

Each begged to take the place of the other. "Spare him. Take me." "No—he's innocent. Kill me instead." The executioner was frozen, the crowd murmuring in disbelief.

Word reached the Emperor. He arrived, stunned by what he saw—two men, each ready to die for the other.

Silence fell as he looked at them, then finally spoke:

"Never in my life have I witnessed such loyalty, such selflessness. You have both proven the very essence of true friendship." *He paused, then smiled.*

"I will spare you both on one condition: that you make me your third friend."

That's why in the Bible, the verse "Love your neighbor like yourself," concludes with "I am God." Because unity and friendship is so precious that even God wants to be part of it. He wants to be the third friend.

When you truly love someone as you love yourself, you wouldn't dream of hurting them—just as you wouldn't harm yourself. That's why the ultimate friendship, marriage, isn't just a partnership; it's a merging of two souls into one. When you see your spouse as an extension of yourself, every word, every action carries weight. You treat them with care, because in doing so, you're also caring for yourself—and no one willingly wounds their own soul.

As with our friends, family and whichever nationality you belong to, as long as you're united, God is with you. If you're divided, you're on our own. People have a tendency to want to help people that help themselves.

Imagine a coworker asks for help moving, and you spend hours hauling boxes while he chats on the phone with his girlfriend, never lifting a finger. Naturally, you'd feel used. And the next time he asks for help? You'd probably tell him to take a hike. No one likes being taken advantage of. When you actively contribute toward what you need, whether it's help, support, or connection, you build a sense of partnership. That effort earns trust, and trust is what turns acquaintances into real friends.

The following story is about the concept of a "half friend." Ask most people how many friends they have, and they might say a few dozen, maybe even a few hundred. Some might admit, "Well, a few are just acquaintances." But no one ever says, "That person is half a friend."

And yet, in reality, many of our relationships live in that fuzzy in-between space. They're not close enough to call at 2 a.m. in a crisis, but not distant enough to call a stranger. These are the people who might cheer us on from the sidelines but disappear when it really matters.

Long ago, there was once a father and son who were discussing friendship.[3] This young man loved to party, surrounded himself with many people and loved to brag about how many friends he had. He boasted to his father, "I have hundreds of true friends."

His father smiled warmly and said, "That's impressive. In all my years, I've only managed to find half a friend."

The son laughed. "Half a friend? How is that even possible?"

His father replied, "It's not that easy to find a true friend. In fact, I'd wager most of yours aren't what they seem. If you'd like, I can give you a test to find out who your real friends are."

---

[3] As heard from Rabbi Noah Weinberg

Intrigued, the son agreed.

"Take a goat," the father said, "slaughter it, put the body in a sack, and smear some of the blood on yourself. Then, in the middle of the night, go to your friends' homes. Tell them you got into a fight at a bar and things went too far— you killed a man. Ask for their help to get rid of the body."

Though shocked by the idea, the son followed his father's instructions. He killed a goat, placed it in a sack, covered himself in blood, and set off to knock on the doors of his so-called friends.

One by one, each of his "friends" turned him away—some in fear, others in anger. None offered to help. Some even threatened to call the authorities. By the end of the night, the young man stood alone, exhausted, humiliated, and disillusioned.

He returned home, dragging the heavy sack behind him, and asked his father, "What now? Not a single one of my 'hundred friends' would help me."

The father nodded and said, "Now, go to my half-friend."

Still bloodied and tired, the son walked to the house of this so-called half-friend and knocked. The man answered the door, and the son repeated the same story.

The man paused, clearly troubled. After a moment, he said, "Although I really shouldn't do this, but you're Chaim's son, so I'll help you."

Without further question, he grabbed a shovel and helped the young man bury the sack deep in the woods.

"Now go back home. Stay out of bars and if someone insults you, just keep quiet. But most of all, forget you even met me."

Shaken, the son returned home and told his father what had happened.

"I don't understand," he said. "Why do you call him only half a friend? He was the only one who helped me!"

The father looked at him kindly and said, "Because a true friend wouldn't say, 'Although I shouldn't do this...' A true friend wouldn't hesitate. A true friend doesn't need to weigh the cost or justify their loyalty. They act—not out of obligation or guilt, but out of unwavering commitment.

This is what a real friend looks like. Now, flip back to the previous chapter and ask yourself: who actually fits that description?

As for the relationships you can't walk away from—family, coworkers, in-laws—the goal isn't to escape them, but to make them as healthy and functional as possible. You may not have chosen those people, but you can choose how you relate and respond to them.

How to Make Relationships Healthy

"Toxic is a chemical classification, not a personality trait"

Now that we've completed our friend audit and nailed down what a real friend actually looks like, you've probably realized you don't have quite as many as you thought. Sorry—not sorry. That's just life. But here's the good news: this uncomfortable little epiphany is the first step toward a much happier and more fulfilling life. You might not believe it if you're still in your 20s, but trust me—when you get older and discover how draining Emotional Vampires are, you'll be thrilled to have fewer people sucking the joy out of your existence.

Now for the people in our lives that are vital, we will delve into how to make these relationships healthy.

Here a few basic concepts to help you set boundaries:

No one needs an all-access pass to your life

Just because you have a phone does not mean you have to answer it.

Just because someone texts you does not mean that you have to respond to it.

Just because you have email does not mean you have to reply to it immediately.

People who are dependent on laying out their emotions on other people will figure a way out to get to you.

Your life is your life. Just because someone now has multiple ways to connect to you wherever you are in the world does not mean you have to connect *back to* everyone at all times. If you keep making yourself available to Emotional Vampires, they will keep making themselves available to *you.*

Learn to put up boundaries for yourself

Boundaries can help you maintain positive mental health. Dysfunction thrives where there is chaos and where there is chaos, boundaries are needed. You have to do your best to make sure that any Emotional Vampires don't come at you with their fangs out ready to suck your emotional health down the drain.

We place boundaries on many things without even thinking about it. Consider your online bank password, a fence around your backyard, or a lock on a gun cabinet. These are all put in place to protect something. Don't you think your mental health is something that you should also protect?

The same thing can be said for physical boundaries. Your body is an altar and not everyone deserves to bow down to it. There is no such thing as casual when your nervous system is that involved. Being physical with another person doesn't just involve a climax—it's a binding contract, written in chemistry and signed with your vulnerability.

We can easily confuse skin-to-skin with heart-to-heart. Then we slap the label "freedom" on it like it's empowerment—but really, it's just a new kind of captivity. One without bars, but with chains you can't see... until it's too late.

The more that a person has access to your inner world, the more responsibility they must demonstrate. Your vulnerability is not free—it takes someone who places a value on your well-being and is worthy enough for you to let them into your inner world.

Many Emotional Vampires feed on emotion, especially Narcissists and Drama Queens. If you don't act emotional to them, there will be no energy for them to feed on. Turbulence in a relationship for a narcissist is like gas is to a car. Without it, they don't function well.

You can't change other people, but you can change your reaction to them. Sometimes silence is the best answer. No one can misquote you or use something against you if you keep your mouth shut.

Here are some simple responses you can use when someone is trying to fight with you or cause you to be emotionally distressed:

- I'll have to think about this.
- I need some time to digest what you said.
- It's best if we don't discuss this when we are emotional.
- We will have to figure out some way to solve this.
- We'll have to agree to disagree.
- I see.
- I'll take your opinion under advisement.
- Or just change the subject.

Here some things that you should not do:

- Don't defend yourself endlessly, you are not going to win.
- Don't explain your every thought.
- Don't try to "win" or make them understand—they don't want to.
- Don't insult or provoke—it just fuels the fire.

Always frame your responses as "I" and not "you." Don't say "You don't yell at me like that." A narcissist will feed off of those responses.

Here are some sample responses:

- I will not respond to those comments.
- I will not listen in that tone of voice.

When the Vampire is a close family member

If your mom calls you everyday and it drains you, then you need to make a boundary.

"Mom, I treasure our talks—but when we go from 'how are you?' to 'let me describe the rash,' it starts to feel like an episode of Grey's Anatomy. I need boundaries: two calls a week, ten minutes each, and absolutely no skin conditions."

Parents can be the hardest ones to have to deal with because most people would like to have their parents in their lives. In addition, you don't want to upset them or tell them the hard truth that they drain you of energy. On the other hand, it can also be an unhealthy relationship that is hard to deal with every week.

The great parenting paradox

Once you understand the following question, it will help you to understand the challenges that parents have.

What is the worst thing your child can ever say to you?

It's not any of the following:

- I hate you
- I wrecked the car last night
- I tattooed my lips
- Please get me out of jail

Believe it or not none of these are the correct answers.

Why?

Because in all of these answers, there is still a relationship. The tattooed lips and jail time means they are calling out for help. The wrecked car means they may not be mature enough to drive. But whatever the case, there is still a relationship.

The answer? I don't need you anymore.

Why is it a paradox?

I have spent my entire married life raising children to be independent, resilient, inquisitive, ambitious and hard working. I want them to take on the world and succeed in whatever they decide to do. Which means, I want them to not need me anymore. The paradox is that I *want* them to need me—I want them to be part of my life. I want them to have my grandkids and be part of *their* lives. This is why it is a paradox. I want to be needed and also want to *not* be needed.

The framework for making those relationships healthier is to identify the issue of what it is that is draining you, especially when the people are your family. Is it:

- Constant criticism?
- Neediness or guilt-tripping?
- Unresolved resentment?
- Lack of boundaries?
- Emotional volatility?

First, you need to define what the word "healthy" means. It doesn't have to mean close. Sometimes it means you just want no drama, to feel emotionally safe, but ultimately you want to be respected. Healthy does not have to mean you eat at your mother's house every week. That only happens for healthy relationships, unless your mom is a Le Cordon Bleu Chef graduate, then you can handle a little drama.

"Healthy" for you may be that you only talk to them once a month and see each other once a year. There are *many* considerations to take into account, such as your spouse, children and how badly your parents drain you. You might need some distance between you to create a healthy dynamic—even if you're still in regular contact.

Boundaries aren't rejection—they're protection for the relationship, because without them, you'll burn out and maybe cut ties entirely. You may have to tell them they need to see a therapist because you can't act as one. You may have to tell a parent that they are causing you mental anguish and it is not healthy for the relationship to continue this way.

Let's learn how to gain a bit more wisdom from the relationship we discussed in an earlier chapter about my mom and sister:

Case Study: *Let me set the scene: I had been dating my future wife for about eight months when we decided to get married. (Side note: I'm pretty sure I knew I wanted to marry her by the second date—I just wasn't mature enough at the time to fully realize it.)*

Naturally, the first step was to have our parents meet. We arranged a brunch so my mother could meet her parents. Her parents were warm, kind, and genuinely sweet—the type of people you instantly feel comfortable around.

My relationship with my mom was... complicated. I loved her deeply, and in many ways, she was a wonderful mother. But maintaining that relationship wasn't always easy. She carried unresolved emotional baggage from her own childhood, which inevitably affected how she raised us. Her love was real, but so were her dysfunctions.

This is where the previous dysfunction between my sister and mother actually helped me make sure it did not happen to me. My father's earlier decision to send my sister to South Florida for school was wise because that is where she met her husband. From the very beginning of my sister's marriage, my mother refused to accept the relationship. It was as if she couldn't allow my sister to be happy.

She wouldn't call my sister by her married name and never fully acknowledged her husband. While they maintained a relationship, it was deeply strained—one-sided and dysfunctional, primarily due to my mother's unresolved emotional issues. My sister endured a lot, but over time, she learned how to manage it. She came to understand that our mother wasn't emotionally well, and she did her best not to take it personally. Watching all of this unfold from the front row gave me clarity. I decided I would never allow that kind of dysfunction to take root in my own life.

So, the day before the brunch where both sets of parents would meet, I sat down with my mom and laid out some very clear boundaries. At this point, I was 35—older and more emotionally mature than most people who marry in their early 20s—so maybe it was a little easier for me to handle.

I told her directly, "I'm marrying into a family with hearts of pure gold. These are kind, thoughtful people who would never say or do anything to hurt anyone. And I won't let anyone bring drama or dysfunction into their family, not even you."

I made it clear: if she brought any of her usual "shtick," whether now or down the road, she would be forfeiting her place in my life and in the lives of her future grandchildren. I wasn't making threats, I was setting boundaries. I told her the choice was entirely hers. I wasn't going to allow history to repeat itself.

In this case, setting clear boundaries turned out to be one of the wisest decisions I ever made. For the rest of my mother's life, she had consistently positive and respectful interactions with my wife, my in-laws, and our children. The dynamic was peaceful and healthy. Something I knew wouldn't have happened without that difficult, but necessary conversation.

If you ever find yourself in a similar situation, laying down ground rules early on is essential, but it must be done with firmness and respect. I told my mother, "I want you in my life, and in the lives of my future wife and children, but only if the relationship is healthy and free of the dysfunction I saw growing up."

And I meant it. I was fully prepared to walk away if needed, and my mother knew I wasn't bluffing. Thankfully, she chose the relationship. As a result, both families enjoyed many years of warm, mutual respect.

Let go of the idea that love means unlimited access. You may have to use limited engagement techniques such as time boxing. This is when you allocate a specific amount of time to your call or visit. It is usually used in a work setting when you want to allocate an amount of time to a specific project. Even though your family isn't a work project, it will work well in these circumstance—okay, maybe some of them are work projects.

You can either warn them in advance of the time limit, or just use excuses when interacting with them that you have to go or get off the phone.

When you do see your parents or siblings, you may have to meet in a neutral place where it would be easier for you to leave if they start to cause problems.

You'll also need to master the art of staying emotionally neutral, or what I like to call ESP: Emotional Separation and Protection.

ESP is all about creating a healthy emotional buffer between you and the person causing you stress. Think of it like putting Rain-X on your car windshield. When it rains, the water doesn't stick—it beads up and slides right off from the wind as you drive—clear vision and no smearing.

Now imagine doing that with family dysfunction. Their comments, drama, or guilt trips will not stick to you anymore. That's the power of ESP. You don't have to absorb every drop of dysfunction. You just need to RainX yourself and your family dysfunction will slide right off of you.

Is this easy to do? Just like anything else in life, it takes some mental prep work. Once you do it, it becomes easier and easier and then you will not dread having to meet your family Vampire for a social event. You'll have your emotional armor on and be prepared for the chaos, dysfunction, criticism, or whatever the Vampire is going to throw your way. This will protect your happiness.

Coach Ratner's Personal Boundaries

It wasn't until I started writing this book that I realized I had been setting boundaries for years—without even knowing that's what I was doing. I was unknowingly acting as the security guard of my own happiness.

Think about it: a police officer wouldn't let a drunk keep driving or a thief walk free after getting caught red-handed… unless, of course, you're in San Fransicko (yes, that's spelled wrong on purpose—calm down).

The point is: boundaries protect us. And once you learn how to put them in place, not only will your relationships improve—you'll be a much happier version of yourself.

Every so often, I get asked to teach a Zoom class. This really only started during the Covid era when suddenly, the world went virtual and pants became optional. I gave it a shot, but it didn't take long to realize: I hate it.

Now, if it were my job and I needed the money, I'd suffer through it like the rest of humanity. But I don't teach for a paycheck, I do it because I genuinely love it. I feed off the energy of a live audience. The bigger the crowd, the more energy I receive, and give back.

I also like to interact—ask questions, get reactions, read the room. You can't do that with a silent grid of muted faces and poor Wi-Fi. There's no spark and almost no feedback. It's less "conversation" and more like performing stand-up comedy for a row of mannequins.

So, I made a decision: I put a fence around my joy. My new rule? No more Zoom classes. It's a boundary I set to protect what I love most—teaching in real life.

Back when I used to travel for coin collector trade shows, I was constantly invited to group dinners with other dealers in my business. When I was new to the trade, I'd always say yes—networking! Connections! Sometimes even free steak!

As I got older (and wiser... and more tired), I realized I actually hate big group dinners. The larger the group, the longer everything takes: from ordering, eating, splitting the check, or debating whether we need another round of appetizers.

And honestly, I started to notice a pattern: a lot of men in my industry are seriously overweight. Why? Giant dinners late at night, followed by collapsing into bed. That's not networking—that's how you get points in a cardiologist's loyalty program.

At the trade shows I used to attend, the day would wrap up around 7pm. But dinner? That was just the beginning of another endurance event. First, everyone heads back to the hotel to freshen up. Then it's a 20-minute walk or a cab ride to the restaurant. By the time we're seated, it's already 9pm. Then come the drinks... the appetizers... dinner... dessert... and because one dessert isn't enough, second dessert.

And just when you think it's over, the bill arrives—and surprise! We're splitting it evenly. That's fun until you realize it includes three bottles of wine that cost anywhere from a few hundred to a few thousand dollars.

Here's the kicker: I'm convinced 90% of people can't tell the difference between a $1,000 bottle of wine and a $25 one from Costco. I got tired of paying for everybody's need to feed their ego so they can look like a wine connoisseur.

Eventually, I had enough. My new rule? If dinner includes more than four people, I'm out. Call it cranky-old-man energy if you want... but trust me, it gets worse from here.

This boundary of mine didn't stop at trade shows—it now fully applies to night weddings. Don't get me wrong, I love weddings—the joy, the dancing! What I don't love is sitting through a three-hour meal, only to be served a lukewarm main course at 11 p.m. So now, whenever one of my students gets married, I tell them the same thing: I'll be there for the ceremony, I'll cry at the vows, but I'm gone before dinner.

Setting that boundary has been a game-changer. It's given me the freedom to protect my energy without the guilt. I get invited to a lot of weddings. That's the perk of having so many students, but late-night meals, three-hour toasts, and dancing to "Hava Nagila" until midnight? I'll take a hard pass. I've reclaimed my evenings, one politely declined slab of kugel at a time.

One important lesson I learned from coin trading—one that saved me a lot of headaches—is how to avoid being taken advantage of. Because I naturally have an empathetic personality, I often found my opinions being used against me.

At conventions, it's common for sellers with interesting collections to walk from table to table, getting offers from different dealers. It's actually a smart strategy. They compare bids and sell to the highest buyer—totally fair and smart business.

If I'm going to invest my time and energy into evaluating a coin deal, I want a fair shot at actually buying it.

So I set a clear boundary.

Before I even look at the coins, I lay out my ground rules: If I make an offer, you have two choices—accept my price, or give me a counter-offer. That's it. If they can't agree to that upfront, I politely decline and won't review the deal at all.

Even if their counter-offer is outrageously high, at least I was given the opportunity to buy the deal. That way, if a colleague ends up closing the deal instead, I don't walk away feeling that I wasted my time. I feel like I got a fair shot.

Setting this boundary has made a big difference. Not only has it boosted my confidence in negotiations, but it has also helped me close more deals. When expectations are clear on both sides, trust goes up—and so does success.

In some cases, dealers run sealed-bid auctions where you have to submit your absolute highest offer—no second chances. If you win, you pay your full bid, not just a small increment over the second-highest offer like you would in a standard public auction (either online or in person).

That's one big advantage to public auctions: they help protect you from overpaying when you misjudge a coin's value. You might bid too high, but you'll usually only pay slightly more than the next person.

But in sealed auctions, there's no such cushion. If anyone makes a mistake and overvalues a coin, which happens to the best of us, they are guaranteed to seriously overpay. That's the gamble.

Here's where things get tricky for me: I'm an aggressive coin buyer. I hate losing a coin—especially one I really want. So if I am always putting down my highest bid, I may buy more coins, but what inevitably happens is I buy the mistakes also. These are the coins that I was too aggressive on, which is usually okay in a public sale because I only have to pay one increment over the previous bid, which means someone else would have had to make the same mistake as me to overpay, which only happens occasionally.

Bidding in a sealed bid auction? There's no safety net. If I overpay, I end up on the losing end of the transaction.

So I stopped doing sealed-bid auctions entirely. Have I been tempted? Absolutely. Sometimes I know there are great coins in those auctions that I'd love to own, and yes, it kills me to pass bidding on them. I've learned the hard way that giving in just leads to regret.

Case Study: *Many years ago, a fellow coin dealer befriended me. Let's call him "Steve," well, because that's his name. He had a lot of issues, but he was also fiercely loyal—the kind of guy who'd take a bullet for you. And honestly, I believe he would totally do it. That kind of loyalty is rare, especially in business. Most people couldn't stand him. I could see why—but I've always made an effort to look for the good in people, it just took a little digging... through several layers of baggage.*

Steve has a case of Obsessive-Compulsive Disorder (OCD) and—possibly—a dash of narcissism—not the most charming cocktail. He always had to be the alpha in the room, which often meant belittling service staff, especially at restaurants. Every time we'd sit down to eat, he'd immediately inspect the silverware for any little spot. One speck on a fork, and he'd summon the waiter and demand replacements with a tone that made me want to apologize on his behalf.

Once, he invited me to dinner at a five-star hotel steakhouse in Las Vegas. He was what the casinos call a "high roller"—the kind of guy who gambles like it's Monopoly money and gets comped rooms, meals, drinks, and probably front row seats to see Carrot Top or Celine Dion if he asked. He said, "I'm taking you to Prime Grill—one of the finest steakhouses in the world. I'll cover the meal; you just take care of the tip. Casinos don't comp tips."

Sounded fair. I was sure it was going to be a memorable meal. After we were served a variety of appetizers, huge steaks, and expensive wine, he ordered cognac for dessert.

Then the bill came.

$2,500.

Steve, of course, reminded me: "I always tip 20%. Don't make me look cheap." (Narcissists only care about what other people think of them.)

That was $500 for me.

Thanks Steve, I really appreciate you taking me out for dinner.

I told Steve that if I ever went out with him again and he complained about anything, that it would be the last time. That is exactly what happened and that ended that, even until today.

Sometimes we need to lay down the rules if we want to be in healthy relationships. But there is another topic that we should discuss before we learn how to find people that we want to be close to us, and that is understanding tolerance versus acceptance.

Tolerance vs Acceptance

There was a local parade recently, advertised as a "Pride and Tolerance" event. I've never been a big fan of the word tolerance—because let's be honest, it sounds more like "I'll put up with you" than "I respect you." Tolerance might keep the peace, but it doesn't build connection. It says, "You can be in the room, but don't expect me to be excited about it." It's a low bar for human interaction—just a notch above ignoring someone entirely.

Tolerance means not agreeing with someone's personal choices—but also recognizing their right to make them. And while tolerance is certainly better than hostility or judgment, it's still a bare minimum. The real goal should be to move beyond tolerance—toward acceptance.

Acceptance doesn't require agreement. It means saying, "I may not fully understand your perspective, but I accept you as a human being with dignity." That mindset creates deeper empathy, and a more respectful society.

We tolerate the racket our kid makes on the drums because it's cheaper than sending them to therapy.

We tolerate politicians whose views make us cringe because elections come around somewhat often.

We even tolerate our partner's emotional unavailability because we make excuses that they'll change.

Tolerance does not demand understanding someone's viewpoint, while acceptance invites someone into your world—acceptance says "come sit with me." Acceptance is rooted in empathy and connection. Acceptance does not mean we have to agree with their viewpoint, because everyone sees things with their own set of goggles. Okay, their goggles may be fogged up and they are not seeing clearly. It may not be our job to clean their goggles, but understanding that their emotions are coming from not seeing clearly will bring you closer to acceptance.

One effective approach to foster understanding and empathy is to view each new person you meet as a 50-chapter book. When you encounter someone—especially in a negative context, or at least from your perspective—you're only witnessing a single chapter of their story. They might be in chapter 25, and you have no insight into the first 24 chapters that shaped who they are today. Perhaps they've experienced emotional trauma or faced challenges you know nothing about. Keeping this perspective in mind can help temper your reactions and judgments. After all, you have no idea what the final chapters of their book will reveal. Their story may culminate in a beautiful, uplifting conclusion!

Can you accept someone without fully agreeing with them? Yes! Otherwise, you will probably never be in a committed loving relationship.

This is why it is important to understand and clarify what the definition of love is. It is the emotional pleasure you feel when you recognize another person's virtues and you continue to appreciate *and* associate them with those virtues throughout your life. To put it another way, everyone has idiosyncrasies, so you better stay focused on why you fell in love in the first place!

Almost anyone you decide to marry is eventually going to cause you some sort of pain—it's an inevitability of relationships. To engage in a passionate relationship you must continually remind yourself of the reasons you chose to marry that person.

This is why only having infatuation for someone will not last. That feeling will eventually go away. You need the infatuation to get you started, but you will need it to evolve into so much more. Unfortunately, many couples lose sight of the qualities that initially attracted them, allowing minor faults to overshadow their partner's virtues.

Consider your children, if you have any. Do they have flaws? Most likely. Yet, no one falls out of love with their children. Even parents of serial murderers may continue to love their children, despite their actions. You don't choose your children, but you are the one that chose your spouse! So why do parents maintain their love for their children, regardless of their behavior, while many are quick to divorce when a spouse's actions disappoint them?

People often get divorced because they lose sight of why they got married in the first place. There were reasons why you fell in love and you got married. What happened to those reasons? Over time, those reasons can fade into the background as you start to focus more on your spouse's flaws, rather than the bond that initially united you.

That's why it's worth learning to shift from simply tolerating people to genuinely accepting them. It doesn't just ease the tension—it deepens your relationships and makes life a whole lot more peaceful in the long run.

If you shift your mindset in marriage and love your spouse the way you love your children, even with all their flaws, you'll create a more passionate and loving relationship.

Unfortunately, many people go through life not on speaking terms with someone closely related. If it's a co-worker, we can tolerate the awkwardness. But when the silence is with someone close—like a parent, sibling, or child—it can take a serious toll on our emotional well-being.

Even those who insist they're fine with the disconnect are often just burying the pain. That unresolved tension has a way of resurfacing, and it may come back to haunt them down the road.

I once heard a powerful suggestion from Rabbi Y.Y. Rubinstein, a well-known international speaker and former BBC Radio broadcaster. He offered a simple but remarkably effective way to begin healing rifts in your personal life—something he said works 99% of the time. Pick up the phone and say quickly: "Don't hang up—this was 100% my fault, and I'd like to apologize in person." More often than not, the other person will hear you out and may even take some responsibility themselves. Sure, there's always a chance they might hang up—but you'll never know unless you try. And that one call could be the first step toward restoring a broken relationship.

Focusing on why we fell in love in the first place is one of the biggest keys to a healthy marriage—even with all their quirks, flaws, and weird habits (yes, even yours). Now take that mindset of focusing on their positive qualities and apply it to everyone else you can't just walk away from. That includes your family, coworkers, and in-laws who think "boundaries" is just another word for "guidelines we'll be ignoring."

This shift can transform the way you handle every relationship. No more cringing at a text from your mother. No more ghosting your sibling's guilt-laced email. No more mentally zoning out while your biggest donor launches into how he prepared for his colonoscopy.

Instead, move from tolerance to acceptance. Use your ESP—Emotional Separation and Protection—for your soul the same way you use RainX for your windshield. Let their dysfunction, drama, anger, and criticism bead up and roll off—so you stay calm, clear, and in control.

And let's be honest: maintaining that connection also gets easier when you master the fine art of apologizing—because you will mess up, especially if you're a man (sorry, guys). The good news is that a sincere, well-delivered apology can get you out of the doghouse faster than flowers, chocolate, or even unloading the dishwasher without being asked.

Not All Apologies Are the Same

"An apology without change is just emotional spam."

Some of the hardest words to say in the English language are:

- I'm sorry
- I forgive you
- I was wrong
- I love you
- Worcestershire sauce

The first 3 are required for healthy relationships. The 4th is needed for a romantic partner, and the last one is great for a ribeye steak!

Admitting you are wrong can seem like a simple thing, but if you are not an empathic person, it can be difficult. Narcissists almost never admit they are wrong and saying that you're sorry—being able to admit you made a mistake, is a healthy emotional response. As we will see, not all admissions of guilt are the same.

There are also times that apologies are not what we need to hear. In Becky Kennedy's Ted talk, an American clinical psychologist and New York Times bestseller of Good Inside, she discusses when we emotionally hurt someone, we may have caused a fracture in the relationship. In that case, that relationship needs repairing *and* an apology.

Sometimes an apology is just a way to shut down the conversation—like saying, 'Hey, I'm sorry I yelled. Can we move on now? Whereas a repair is going back to a point of disconnection, taking responsibility for your behavior and acknowledging the impact it had on someone else.

Imagine a water pipe with a fracture in it. Some water may trickle through to the end faucet, but most of the water will seep into the ground and be wasted. The same can be said for a relationship.

Get good at repairing relationships. Although it's always better to throw in an apology, that can always come later.

Tell yourself that you are getting good at focusing on repair. Understand that it's a 2 step process. First you rupture, then you repair. You make a mistake (and then never do it again), and then you fix it.

When someone ruptures their relationship, the guilty person is now a different person in the eyes of the one that got hurt. They now look at them as a scary friend, sibling, or partner. They can also be a scary mom or dad. The hurt person is going into a state of distress and they have to find a way to feel safe and secure again. And if the perpetrator does not repair this, who do they blame? They may rely on the only coping mechanism that they have at their disposal. Self-blame.

Something's wrong with me.

I'm unloveable.

I make bad things happen.

While self-blame can work for us in childhood and we usually get over it, we all know it works against us in adulthood. These are core fears of so many adults. But really, these are the childhood stories we wrote when we were left alone following stressful events that went without repair. Adults with self blame are vulnerable to depression, anxiety and self-worthlessness.

When we can retell stories from our past that caused us distress, but now tell them in a safe environment, the story changes…and we change. With repair, we effectively change the past. This is what good therapy does.

Self-repair means separating your identity from your behavior.

My latest behavior does not define me.

I was a good parent that was having a bad day.

I was a good partner, but my anger got the best of me.

I am not a bad person, I just did not have the proper tools to respond in a healthy way.

After you take responsibility and repair, state what you would do differently the next time.

A 15 second intervention can have a lifelong impact. You can replace someone's story of self-blame with a story of self trust, safety and connection. What an awesome upgrade!

These are NOT repair:

"I am sorry I yelled at you, but if you were more grateful, then I wouldn't get mad at you."

"I am sorry I smacked you, but if you would have listened the first time, this would not have happened"

They all insinuate that someone else caused your reaction, which is not a model of emotional regulation we want to pass off on the next generation.

It's never too late to repair a fractured relationship.

Once you do, you will need to make an apology that is honest, caring, and real. The following are a list of a variety of types of apologies. Not all of them are the same and you will see that they all have different meanings.

The Simple Apology

"Sorry about that!" This is the casual sorry for small inconveniences or social niceties—like bumping into someone or being slightly late. It shows awareness, but not much emotional investment. It's the apology that 6 year olds use whose parents make them say "sorry" to their little sister for pouring a bucket of sand over their head.

The Apology w/ Justification

"I'm sorry, but…" At first, this may sound like an apology, but it falls short of being genuine. It often sidesteps true responsibility, especially when the other person feels hurt and is seeking real ownership. The word "but" signals a shift away from accountability, suggesting that the apology is conditional or that blame is being placed elsewhere. Instead of expressing sincere remorse, it becomes an attempt to excuse or minimize the harm caused.

The Partial Apology

"I'm sorry I upset you." This level recognizes the emotional impact, but may not fully admit fault or show understanding of what went wrong. In this version, the person apologizing doesn't really mean they are sorry, only that they are sorry that what they did may have hurt the other person. In their mind, they may be completely innocent.

The Avoiding Conflict Apology

Sometimes, a person will say "I'm sorry" just to avoid conflict, even when they believe they've done nothing wrong. This dynamic often shows up in marriage, where one spouse apologizes simply to keep the peace. Used occasionally and with some wisdom, this kind of apology can help de-escalate tension and maintain harmony. However, when it becomes a pattern—where one partner is constantly apologizing just to avoid anger or to keep the other calm—it's no longer healthy. In fact, it may be a red flag for emotional manipulation, or even abuse. In a balanced relationship, both partners should feel safe expressing their perspective without fear of emotional fallout.

The Instant Apology

One where you are speaking and immediately realize you said something wrong and apologize before the other person can even show their negative emotions. This is usually done during an argument with a close loved one.

The Apology to Get Food, Sex, or Money

Then there's the apology that comes with strings attached—when someone says "I'm sorry" primarily because they want something from you. While the apology might be sincere, it's often clouded by the fact that they stand to gain from your forgiveness. This creates a lingering doubt: Are they truly remorseful, or just trying to get what they want? When an apology is motivated by self-interest, it can still be valid, but it's harder to trust.

The Fake Apology While Taking Responsibility

"I'm sorry I said that. What I said hurt you and I did not mean to do that.»

Although in your apology you said you didn't mean to do it, in reality, you *did* mean to do it and it hurt the other person.

The Real Apology While Taking Responsibility

"I'm sorry I said that. What I said hurt you and I did not mean to do that." In this instance, the person is admitting guilt and telling them that they were acting on emotions and it was not their true feelings. Here, the person is taking real accountability, and expressing empathy. This apology and the one above are the same. It takes reading someone's facial expressions to know if it is a real apology or a fake one.

The Full Apology with Responsibility with Empathy

"I deeply regret what I did. I was wrong, and I hurt you. You didn't deserve that, and I want to correct it."

This is the most sincere level—it includes vulnerability, remorse, emotional connection, and often a desire to change or make amends.

***Case study:** One of my students attended a singles dinner where a guy she was supposed to go out with happened to be at the same table. She told me he was rude and dismissive toward her the entire evening, and after that, she had zero interest in giving him a shot. His friends tried to smooth things over, saying she should give him a second chance* *because "he was just drunk." She asked for my advice, and I told her flat-out: being drunk isn't an excuse—in fact, it's a tell-tale sign of someone's true self. When the liquor flows, the truth shows. Alcohol doesn't hide character— it reveals it. If that's who he becomes with a drink in his hand, then that's someone you probably don't want holding your hand.*

Alcoholics are notorious for apologizing for their behavior after the damage has been done. Who out there wants to marry a bad drunk? I don't see any hands raised. While apologies may be the first step, real healing between two people only begins when forgiveness enters the picture.

3 Levels of Forgiveness

*"When saying 'I'm fine'
is just emotional duck tape."*

I f your favorite hobby is collecting every injustice ever done to you, I've got a better suggestion, and no, it's not collecting Taylor Swift friendship bracelets; try coins instead. Not only have collectible coins consistently outpaced inflation, but they're also far more fun than stockpiling injustices. More importantly, collecting something meaningful can actually boost your emotional well-being. So stop blaming everyone and everything for your misery. Start investing in something that pays off—especially in peace of mind.

Constantly bottling up emotional pain doesn't make it disappear—it just weighs you down over time. When you choose to forgive, letting them off the hook is not your #1 goal—it's letting yourself off the hook. Forgiveness lifts the burden and frees you to focus on the good in your life instead of being trapped by the past.

In *Before Forgiveness: The Origins of A Moral Idea* (2010), a fascinating recent book by an American Classics professor, David Konstan, he argues that there was no concept of forgiveness in the literature of the ancient Greeks. There was something else, often mistaken for forgiveness—it is appeasement of anger.

The Greek word *sungnome*, sometimes translated as forgiveness, really means, says *Konstan, exculpation* or *absolution*. It is not that I forgive you for what you did, but that I understand why you did it—you couldn't really help it, you were caught up in circumstances beyond your control—or, alternatively, I do not need to take revenge because you have now shown that you hold me in proper respect. My dignity has been restored.

In Jewish tradition, forgiveness isn't just a virtue, it's a foundational theme woven throughout the Bible. Two powerful stories illustrate what genuine forgiveness truly looks like.

The first takes place at Mount Sinai. As Moses receives the Torah, the people below lose patience and build the infamous golden calf. God's initial response is fierce—many perish by plague or the sword. Yet, astonishingly, the nation as a whole is forgiven. God renews His covenant with them, and the relationship between the people and their Creator is restored. This moment teaches us that while forgiveness may come with consequences, it is still possible—even after betrayal.

The second story offers perhaps an even deeper lesson and is portrayed in the Broadway musical, Joseph and the Amazing Technicolor Dreamcoat. During a time of famine, the sons of Jacob travel to Egypt in search of food. They unknowingly stand before their long-lost brother Joseph, whom they had sold into slavery two decades earlier. When Joseph finally reveals his identity, the narrative takes an unexpected turn. There is no revenge. There is no grudge. And most astonishingly, there isn't even a hint of passive-aggressive forgiveness.

Instead, Joseph completely releases his brothers from blame. He tells them that everything that happened—including their betrayal—was orchestrated by God for a greater purpose: to save lives and ensure the survival of their family. "It was not you who sent me here," Joseph says, "but God."

If the world could internalize this level of humility and commitment to forgiveness, we would be living in messianic times. Joseph didn't just forgive, he elevated the entire concept of forgiveness, showing us what it means to live above resentment and to see the hand of God even in our deepest pain.

The great medieval Jewish philosopher and Torah commentator, Rambam (Moses ben Maimon, aka Maimonides), explains in his Laws of Repentance that forgiveness operates on three distinct levels:

1. External Forgiveness: Forgiving the action, not the sinner. When one person wrongs another, the victim may forgive the offense, but not the offender.

In doing so, they often cling to a hidden grudge, which will fuel inner turmoil. Holding on to this grudge doesn't punish anyone, except the heart of the one who harbors it. True peace comes not from partial forgiveness, but from releasing the person entirely. If you want to live a life of emotional serenity, offer full forgiveness to the one who committed it.

2. Internal Forgiveness: Forgiving the action and partially the sinner. A higher level of forgiveness is to forgive not just the act of sin, but also the guilty person, even though there still may remain a trace of dislike for the person. There's still some healing to do, even if the pain hasn't fully disappeared. Hopefully, someday, you will eventually get to full reconciliation.

3. Full Reconciliation: This is the highest and most complete form of forgiveness. This level is an emotion so strong that it makes it as if they never occurred at all. This is the kind of forgiveness that matters most in a romantic relationship. At this level, the relationship is not only restored, but strengthened; it transforms itself into greater connection with the person you forgave.

In Jewish law, a person is only obligated to ask for forgiveness three times. After three refusals, the person is no longer held accountable for that action, as they have proven their true regret. At that point, the burden shifts: the one who refuses to forgive is now considered to be bearing a grudge.

This is the level of forgiveness that God offers on the Jewish holiday of Yom Kippur for those who have sincerely repented.

Rambam's framework shows that forgiveness isn't just a switch we flip—it's a process, one that requires humility. But as we grow in our ability to forgive, we not only free others, we free ourselves.

A teacher stands before her class, arm outstretched, holding a bottle of water in her hand. She asks the students, "How much do you think this bottle weighs?" Answers range from six ounces to a pound. She smiles and says, "The exact weight doesn't matter. What matters is how long I hold it." She explains, "If I hold it for a minute, it's light. If I hold it for an hour, my arm will ache. If I hold it all day, it will feel unbearable. Yet the weight never changed—only the length of time I carried it." She pauses, letting the lesson sink in. "This is what happens when we hold on to grudges or refuse to forgive. The pain doesn't come from the weight itself, but from carrying it too long."

If you still have a hard time forgiving, you are just holding a grudge. Find something else to collect instead of all the injustices done to you; you'll be a much happier person…even if it's Taylor Swift friendship bracelets.

Find Your Keepers

*"Jeepers creepers,
where'd ya get those peepers?"*

I love using acronyms in all my classes and books. Why? Because wisdom isn't worth much if you can't remember it when it counts. An acronym locks an idea into your memory, making it easy to access when life throws you a contradiction or you're faced with a tough decision.

Think of it like your computer with a bunch of tabs open—you keep them there because you want quick access when you need them. Acronyms work the same way for your brain. They're mental shortcuts to wisdom and keep the good stuff just one mental click away.

The acronym for KEEPER is one you can refer to in many circumstances. You can use it when you are deciding whether to go on a date, which friends you want to spend time with, or even use it as parents when trying to teach your kids to develop great character traits. Let's be honest, "clean your room" only goes so far.

While many of the qualities of a KEEPER are valuable in all personal relationships—friendships, business connections, and family—they are absolutely essential in marriage. And even though this book isn't specifically about marriage, I'd bet that if you asked most people, single or not, whether they'd want a successful, passionate, loving relationship, the answer would be a resounding yes.

The truth is, when someone says they don't want to get married, it's often not because they don't value connection. It's because, deep down, they fear vulnerability. They're not sure they can truly open their heart to someone else, and that fear disguises itself as indifference. But at our core, most of us long for love, we just have to feel safe enough to receive it.

That's why it's so important to make sure your social circle is free of Emotional Vampires because if you learn to spot them early in friendships, you'll be far less likely to marry one. Healthy relationships start with healthy patterns, and it all begins with the company you keep.

We have many different kinds of relationships and each one has a different dynamic that we should be aware of. All relationships are deeply interconnected so understanding one category can provide valuable insights into another. When you strengthen one area, you often see a ripple effect in the others. In my view, there are four key relationship categories that shape our lives:

- Self (self-esteem)
- Spouse or partner (dating and marriage)
- Children (parenting)
- Friends, acquaintances, and family (The focus of this book)

You could also include work relationships in the mix, but let's be honest, there are already enough books out there about toxic workplaces to fill an HR department. So for now, I've decided to leave that category off the list.

One theme I often teach is this: you are generally only as happy as your worst relationship. While this isn't always 100% accurate, there is a significant amount of truth to it. We all have people in our lives who drain our energy. Recognizing these relationships and learning how to navigate them wisely can help us maintain kindness, respect, and ultimately our happiness—not just toward others, but most importantly, toward ourselves.

Since this book is about helping you lead a more emotionally happy and healthy life, it would be incomplete if I didn't give you tools to recognize the kind of people who actually add to your well-being. After all, emotional health isn't just about managing your own stuff, it's also about choosing the right people to do life with.

Remember the woman in the beginning of this book who was draining our family of healthy energy? My wife decided that she needed to make a boundary in her life for the difficult people, so, she came up with an acronym that perfectly captures the kind of person she wants to surround herself with. It might just help you do the same.

She calls them *KEEPERs*

- **K**ind
- **E**go
- **E**nvy
- **P**eaceful
- **E**mpathic
- **R**espectful

Of course, not all of the traits listed above are ones we want in our lives. So the first step is easy: we eliminate two of the E's—**E**nvy and **E**go.

Those are deal-breakers, not Keepers.

- **K**ind
- ~~**E**go~~
- ~~**E**nvy~~
- **P**eaceful
- **E**mpathic
- **R**espectful

Ego

If you discover that your friend has an inflated ego, don't be surprised when they start draining the life out of you. People with oversized egos tend to think the world revolves around them—and if you stick around long enough, you may become one of their moons.

Big egos often go hand in hand with narcissism. These are the folks who take all the credit, none of the blame, and somehow turn every conversation back to themselves.

Interestingly, ego is also an acronym: E.G.O. = Exiting God Out. It reflects the mindset that says, "I'm in control, I'm self-made, I'm the reason everything in my life works." There's no room for humility, gratitude, or even the slightest nod to the idea that their talents were gifts—given at birth, not earned at the gym or at a Tony Robbins convention.

It's like someone winning the lottery and bragging about their investing skills. Ego isn't just annoying—it's spiritually blind. Because when you forget the Giver, you misuse the gift.

Let's be honest—no one likes someone with an overinflated ego. It's not confidence; it's often just low self-esteem wearing a superman cape. And this puffed-up persona poses one of the biggest threats to our relationships. Ego shows up everywhere: in the car we drive, the house we live in, the job titles we chase, and sometimes, in the partners we pick.

Take, for example, the classic case of the wealthy older man dating someone young enough to be his granddaughter. Let's not kid ourselves—this usually isn't about a deep emotional connection. It's about walking into a restaurant and thinking, "Look at me, world!" It's just a flashy attempt to fill a void where inner fulfillment should be. It's less about love and more about needing a life size 22 year old blonde trophy.

When we feel insecure, we often try to look important instead of being important.

One thing our ego likes to do is to make ourselves look good. Why? We feel good about ourselves when we're told we look good. Who doesn't like that? But when that affirmation doesn't come, especially from your partner, your ego starts fishing for attention, either by over-posting on Instagram, or suddenly developing a passion for shirtless selfies.

Here's the truth: your ego is not your amigo. It might dress things up nicely on the outside, but it won't lead you to deeper friendships, more passionate marriages, or better parenting.

At best, it gets you likes; at worst, it gets you lonely.

One of the best ways to deflate an overinflated ego is to recognize a simple truth: every skill, talent, or ability you have is a gift. You didn't manufacture it—you were born with it. Whether you're crushing it in real estate, running a successful business, or training for the Olympic team, those abilities are rooted in gifts from the start. Yes, you're using your God-given skills, but don't forget who gave them to you in the first place.

Think of this idea that every person is given an imaginary check as soon as they are born. Everyone has a check for a different amount of money. Yours may be $5,000 and your best friend's may be $10,000. These imaginary checks we are given determine how much potential we have in this world. Now ask yourself: Would you ever take your $5,000 check to the bank and ask the teller, "Just give me $4,000 and keep the change"? Of course not! That is exactly what you are doing when you don't reach your potential in life.

We should all strive to become the greatest version of ourselves. Recognizing and developing the talents and skills we've been given is how to do that—by turning potential into purpose, and ability into achievement, in every area of life. When one is arrogant about their qualities in life, they are just using their God given skills—they are just cashing their check.

***Case Study:** In the rare coin business, the field I work in, you'll find no shortage of movers and shakers. Many people in this industry start earning significant incomes early in their careers. Before long, they're driving luxury cars, wearing Rolexes, and taking lavish vacations. But success like that can be dangerous if you're not mentally and emotionally prepared for it. It often goes to their heads, inflating their egos. Then, when they face real challenges, whether financial setbacks or personal relationship struggles, they're not equipped to handle them. At the root of this imbalance is a lack of gratitude.*

True gratitude means recognizing that your talents and skills are a gift—not something you manufactured on your own. That mindset keeps your ego grounded and your perspective healthy. This phenomenon isn't limited to the coin world—it's similar to what happens with professional athletes straight out of college. They sign multi-million dollar contracts but often struggle to sustain that lifestyle long-term, simply because they weren't prepared for what success demands on the inside.

Envy

The second E stands for Envy. Envy is an emotion that occurs when you want something that someone else has—whether it's their success, possessions, talents, looks, or even relationships.

It often comes with feelings of resentment or frustration, like:

"Why do they have that and I don't?"

"They don't deserve that; I should have it instead."

Having a person in your life who has envy of others may bring you down to their level of unhappiness. It shows that they are never satisfied with what they have in life. This will be a constant drain the closer they are to you.

It suggests that the world is not working in the way that they would like.

"I don't have that job, wife, money, body, house, or car, and I would be much happier if I had it!"

There is an ancient saying that bodes well for people to internalize in today's materialistic infested world, "Who is rich? One who is happy with their lot in life." This is more than a quote—it's a life-changing mantra.

Envy steals joy and replaces it with endless longing. But contentment—true gratitude for what you already have—creates lasting happiness. Surround yourself with people who are thankful, not envious. Because envy doesn't just steal joy from the envious—it drains the joy from everyone around them

So now that we have removed people that are envious and have over inflated egos, we are left with 4 character traits of the people we want in our life *and* want to spend time with: **K**ind, **P**eaceful, **E**mpathetic, and **R**espectful.

- **K**ind
- **P**eaceful
- **E**mpathic
- **R**espectful

Kind

Kindness is one of the most essential qualities in any meaningful relationship. Truly kind people look out for others, especially their friends. They don't keep score or measure how much they've given versus what they've received. When you're going through a hard time, they're the ones who respond to your texts right away—not days later. They show up when it matters.

Kind people don't help with strings attached, and they don't expect anything in return. They don't speak badly about others or engage in gossip. Instead, they quietly lift people up, offer support without being asked, and are always looking for ways to make someone else's life a little better.

Case study: *When I was teaching a class on kindness, I asked the room, "How many of you did something kind for someone else this week?" Almost every hand shot up. Then I followed up: "Great—can you share something specific you did?" Suddenly, every hand went down.*

That's when I pointed out the truth: they were kind in theory, but not in practice. Real kindness isn't just a mindset—it requires action. It takes effort, intention, and follow-through. Without that, kindness remains just a nice idea, not something that actually makes a difference in the world.

When I'm giving advice to young people who are dating, one of the most common questions I get is: "What's the most important character trait to look for in a spouse?" I always say that emotional health is absolutely essential—and right behind it is kindness. Kindness can compensate for a lot of other flaws. Someone who is kind will be patient, compassionate, and supportive—and that can make even the toughest parts of marriage easier to navigate.

You can often see a person's true character in how they treat people in the hospitality industry. If someone is rude to a waiter or waitress, that's a serious red flag—and a clear warning sign that this may not be the kind of person you want to build a relationship with. Ignoring those red flags is one of the fastest ways to end up in a toxic relationship.

On the flip side, if someone shows kindness and respect to those in more vulnerable or service-oriented roles, it's a strong indication they'll treat others well too—especially those they're close to.

You also need to be kind to yourself—and that starts with clarity. If you're not clear on why you're dating, you're setting yourself up to choose the wrong person for the wrong reasons. It's one of the biggest mistakes people make, often prioritizing chemistry over character—and paying the price later.

Just imagine a young single 22 year old woman, beautiful and charismatic. She is the kind of person many men are attracted to. If you ask her why she is dating, she might casually reply, "Guys ask me out all the time, and I like the attention." And this is where a major mistake begins. Press her a little further—ask her to clarify why she's dating—and she'll likely pause, shrug, and say something like, "I don't know... I'm just seeing where it goes."

I can tell you where it's going to go—right into the toilet!

Without a clear purpose, dating becomes a game of chance instead of a meaningful search for compatibility and connection.

Here are some of the reasons why people start dating:

- To find a spouse and get married
- To have a physical or intimate relationship
- To have someone to go out with—dinners, movies, events
- Simply because they don't want to feel alone

These are just a few possible reasons people start dating, but here's where the problem begins: if you don't clearly define your intentions, you risk confusing infatuation with love. And that confusion can lead you down the wrong path. Fast forward five years into a marriage, and you may find yourself wondering how you ended up in a toxic or unfulfilling relationship.

Here's how it often plays out: a woman meets a decent guy, and once physical intimacy enters the relationship, both of them start making decisions based more on emotion than intellect. Over time, as they grow familiar and comfortable with each other, they decide to get married—often with the shared goal of starting a family. But unfortunately, many of these marriages don't last. Why? Because the foundation was built more on emotional momentum than on intentional, value-driven choices.

Failure in marriage doesn't always mean it ends in divorce. Sometimes, failure looks like two people staying together for decades—yet no longer being passionately in love. A marriage can technically last "until death do us part," but that doesn't necessarily make it a success. It may simply be a long, quiet story of dysfunction, disconnection, or emotional emptiness.

This creates the perfect storm for what's known as an "empty nest divorce." When a couple builds their marriage solely around raising children. Once those children grow up and leave, the foundation of the relationship disappears. With their shared purpose gone, they may suddenly realize there's nothing holding them together anymore.

If you're dating with the goal of marriage, then after a few weeks—or at most a couple of months—you should have a clear sense of whether this person is marriage material.

Maybe it is possible that some people need a year or two to decide, but generally they are not being honest about their intentions, or they are a 2nd guesser, unsure about their decisions.

If the person you are dating is unkind or showing danger signs, end the relationship and move on. If you still can't decide after that time, it likely means you're either unclear about what you truly want, or you're willfully ignoring warning signs that shouldn't be overlooked.

Ignoring warning signs usually stems from a lack of clear intent, or more commonly, from fear. Many people worry that no one else will want them, so they stay in the relationship, hoping the toxicity will somehow disappear. Unfortunately, it rarely does. In fact, those issues tend to intensify, especially after marriage.

True kindness is when someone does something for you without expecting anything in return. It's selfless, sincere, and rare. But be cautious—especially early in a relationship—when acts of kindness may come with hidden motives. The same applies to salespeople, fundraisers, or anyone who stands to gain from your trust. Genuine kindness doesn't come with strings attached.

When a young person takes the time to clarify why they're dating, they're far less likely to fall into the trap of marrying someone who isn't right for them. It's surprisingly easy to grow comfortable with someone who doesn't treat you kindly. Over time, you begin justifying their behavior, and before you know it, you're walking down the aisle—without ever gaining the clarity needed to realize they weren't marriage material. Why does this happen? Because you got emotionally attached first and only thought about marriage later. In my view, this backwards approach is one of the biggest reasons so many marriages struggle—or fail entirely.

How many people do you know who are divorced or stuck in unhappy relationships and now say, "I wish I had seen the red flags earlier"? The truth is, the signs were there—they just chose not to see them.

You might have a friendship that began back in school, but now you're starting to see that this person isn't all that kind. You hesitate to end the friendship because of your shared history. While it's not as serious as marrying the wrong person, keeping unkind people in your life can quietly drain your happiness. Surrounding yourself with genuinely kind individuals is one of the best things you can do for your emotional well-being.

Peaceful

Peace in any relationship isn't a luxury—it's a requirement. Why keep someone in your life who constantly stirs up tension? Unless you're married to them, there's no reason to tiptoe around someone worrying that your next word or move might trigger criticism or rage.

Your peace of mind should be non-negotiable. If someone consistently brings chaos, drama, or emotional whiplash, it's time to say, "Thanks, but no thanks." Protecting your peace means giving yourself permission to eject the people who keep disturbing it.

You might find yourself dating someone with anger issues—and at first, you make excuses. You tell yourself, "They're just stressed," or "Everyone has a bad day now and then." And during dating, it's easier to tolerate because you're only spending limited time together. But marriage? That's a whole different story.

When you live with someone, anger doesn't just show up occasionally—it moves in with you. Suddenly, you're tiptoeing around the house, constantly on edge, thinking, "When is this person going to lose it?" What feels manageable while dating becomes exhausting—and ultimately, intolerable—when it's part of your daily life.

Being peaceful doesn't mean we have to agree on everything. As mentioned earlier in the book, healthy relationships allow room to agree to disagree. Peace is about mutual respect, not identical opinions.

There are countries in the world who have peace treaties. These treaties are made so that each country can function without having to worry about sneak attacks from the other. It does not mean they like each other. Peace can also just mean absence of war. Obviously, this is not the kind of peace we want with our romantic partner, but we certainly can make that work if it is a co-worker or classmate.

Surrounding yourself with peaceful people can significantly reduce anxiety and guide you toward a life of emotional balance and serenity. The people you choose matter—and choosing peace is choosing sanity.

Empathic

As we discussed earlier in the book, narcissists tend to feed off empathetic people. Why? Because narcissists are takers and empaths are givers. It's a one-way street that leads to emotional burnout. So ask yourself honestly: which type do you want in your life—the one who drains you, or the one who fills you up?

Empaths genuinely find joy in giving to others. Unlike the other categories of Emotional Vampires, they don't drain your emotional energy, they actually help protect it. Why? Because they're deeply sensitive to the feelings of those around them. These are the people who uplift, support, and bring calm—not chaos. In short, this is the kind of person you want in your life.

Respectful

The people you surround yourself with should respect your time, your energy, and everything you bring to the table. In a romantic relationship, one of the most important questions a woman should ask herself before marrying a man is: Do I truly respect him?

Respect is the foundation of any strong marriage, for both parties, but definitely more for a man. You need to accept your partner for who they are—because odds are, they're not going to change much after the wedding. If you're not happy with who they are now, you probably won't be happy later either. Sure, your future spouse may promise to improve, and they might even mean it, but building a lifelong commitment on potential is risky. You are going to marry the person in front of you, not the version you hope they'll become.

Let's consider a scenario where you believe your future husband engages in some immature activities—like spending hours in his basement playing video games or building toothpick houses. If this bothers you now and you're thinking, "It's just a phase... he'll grow out of it once we're married." Spoiler alert: he won't. It's unlikely that those feelings will simply vanish after marriage. If you expect that he will abandon his hobbies once you're married, you may find yourself disappointed. What you see is what you get—with slightly more laundry.

It's essential to recognize that this is how he enjoys spending his free time, and respecting his interests is crucial. Accepting each other's hobbies and quirks is a key part of building a healthy relationship.

Suppose your potential husband wants to go to law school so he can become a partner at a major law firm. This ambition will likely involve long hours of studying and busy weekends, leaving less time for family. He may expect you to handle household responsibilities alone while he focuses on his studies. If you choose to marry him, it's essential that you respect his decision.

In many of my private coaching sessions, young women often share that they feel unsure about marrying the man they're dating. I ask them directly, 'Do you respect him?' If they hesitate or avoid eye contact, it's a clear sign that an underlying issue is troubling them. If it is important to respect your spouse, it is also just as important that anyone in your life should respect you. If they don't, they don't reach the level of being a KEEPER.

Only Kind, Peaceful, Empathic, and Respectful people make the cut on your team. Ego and Envy are red flags—deal-breakers, not keepers. Emotional health starts by cleaning up your circle. If you can spot Emotional Vampires early on—especially in friendships—you're much less likely to end up married to one.

Closing

In one of my classes, a student once suggested that I should add an "S" to KEEPER and make it KEEPERS. Then the S should stand for self-esteem. After thinking it over, I told them—I don't actually think high self-esteem is a must-have for everyone in your life. Let's be clear: I'm not saying you should marry someone with low self-esteem—that's a whole different dynamic, and marriage requires a different emotional foundation.

However, when it comes to friends or family? I've got plenty of people in my life who struggle with self-esteem issues, and I genuinely enjoy their company. Not everyone needs to walk around radiating confidence like a TED Talk speaker. Some of the kindest, most thoughtful people are the ones still figuring themselves out—and they're often far more pleasant to be around than someone with an ego so large it needs its own zip code.

Emotional Vampires on the other hand? They don't just bite your neck—they drain your joy and maybe even your sanity. You only get one life—why waste it with people you don't enjoy spending time with? Once you become aware of who's sapping your energy, you gain the power to protect your emotional health.

Keep the Emotional Vampires out of your life, and you'll instantly feel lighter—like you just dropped a 50-pound backpack. No one needs their joy sucked out of them like a Capri Sun at summer camp: let the Keepers in, kick the Vampires out.

You're the gatekeeper to your happiness—not everyone deserves the key.

Boom.

About the Author

Coach Ratner is a passionate speaker and writer on relationships, self-esteem, and spirituality. A successful entrepreneur turned personal growth expert, he now shares his hard-earned wisdom to help others live more meaningful and empowered lives.

To bring Coach Ratner to your organization or event, reach out at CoachRatner@gmail.com. Catch his insights on The Coach Ratner Podcast, available on Apple, Spotify, or wherever you get your podcasts.

You can also visit him on Youtube, CoachRatner.com or attend his weekly public classes at the Aish World Center in the Old City of Jerusalem—where inspiration comes with a view.

Preview for

When Botox Meets Bezos

Where Low Self-Esteem and Plastic Surgery Collide

Did you see those Bezos–Sánchez wedding photos from the summer of 2025? You could've mistaken it for the grand opening of a Beverly Hills med spa. With that kind of money flying in on over 90 private jets, most of those guests had no problem swiping their black Amex to pay for breast enhancements, Botox, and enough dermal filler to make Lisa Rinna's pout look thin. But here's the irony—when all is said and done, spending all that money with plastic may leave you looking like plastic.

I understand that this title may be a bit edgy, but some things are just too obvious not to say out loud. I really wanted to title the book, "How to Prevent Another Bezos Divorce". And no, I'm not talking about Jeff Bezos's first wife, MacKenzie Scott—who, for the record, is already two divorces in. I'm talking about Jeff Bezos himself: founder of one of the most valuable companies on the planet and one of the richest men alive, depending on that day's closing price of Amazon stock.

I *can't* be the only one in the room who looked at the pictures from their wedding in Venice in the summer of 2025 and thought to myself, there is *no* chance that this is going to last.

How long does the average wedding last? Four hours, maybe five, max. This one lasted for 3 days! Yet there is no correlation between how long your wedding lasts and how long your marriage lasts. You could spend $50 million on flowers, hire Adele to sing you down the aisle, and have Gordon Ramsay scream at your caterers all night and your marriage could still tank faster than Brad Pitt and Jennifer Aniston.

Have you heard anyone ever say, "Thank God for our over-the-top wedding party, otherwise my marriage would have never lasted."

These are words that you will never hear.

What's the first thing someone does as soon as they get engaged? They call their parents, or maybe in the Bezo/Sanchez situation, they call their children. "Congratulations" is heard through the phone, but who is the very next call going to be to? The wedding planner! The next six month are spent on deciding who is going to make the "A" list and deciding on how you are going to let down the crazy relatives that you really don't want to come. Then there's the reception to organize—choosing the caterer, photographer, band, color scheme, venue, date, and menu. Some brides go to great lengths, traveling across the country to be fitted for an Oscar de la Renta gown or Christian Louboutin shoes that they'll only wear once. In fact, many brides spend more on a wedding dress than some people spend on their entire wedding! While these details may seem crucial at the moment, they pale in comparison to the significance of building a lasting marriage.

What is the last scene in any romantic comedy movie you have ever watched? It's usually the wedding. Why don't they ever show what happens after 10, 20, or 30 years after the wedding? Because it would not be a romantic comedy—it would be a murder mystery! The day you get married is the day your marriage starts!

Everyone walking down the aisle is going into it thinking that it is going to last forever. Yet, rarely does it ever get to "until death do us part."

If you take 100 marriages in the United States today—either billionaire marriages or just regular people—how many get divorced? Let's say that it's about 50. This means that there are 50 marriages still left. Now out of those 50, how many do you think are in happy, passionate, loving relationships? I used to say about half, but after teaching thousands of students over the last few years, it appears to be much worse than I thought. Just being married to the same person your whole life doesn't automatically mean the marriage is a success.

Out of the 50 left that are still married, maybe 10 are in a relationship of passionate wedded bliss—and that's probably being generous.

This means as you are walking down the aisle to get married, you have a 10% chance that this marriage will be successful.

Seriously, that really stinks.

Now you understand the purpose of this book—it's to make sure *you* don't make the same mistake that unfortunately, many other people do, including the richest men in the world. We are going to discuss how to counteract the many mistakes people make when choosing their spouse.

Marriage does not have to be difficult if you go into it with the proper wisdom. Everyone *thinks* they know what they are doing when they are walking down the aisle to tie the knot, but they may not have the wisdom. Unfortunately, there is a big difference between wisdom and knowledge. Knowledge is knowing that tomato is a fruit, wisdom is knowing not to put it into a fruitcake. If you give your whole heart to someone without the right wisdom, you're not just taking a risk—you're the fruitcake.

Don't be a fruitcake.

This book is going to delve into the wisdom that you need to have a passionate marriage with one person the rest of your life. Jeff Bezos has probably not read this book. Hopefully he will, but I doubt he has the time or wherewithal to, but that does not mean *you* don't have to.

The only difference between you, the reader, and Jeff Bezos, is he owns a private jet—okay maybe 4 private jets, but who's counting.

One of the reasons I started writing books on relationships is because, after about 10 years of marriage, I turned to my wife and said, "Why is our marriage good, but not great—just like everybody else's?" I mean, many marriages are full of dysfunction: infidelity, narcissism, gaslighting, abuse... meanwhile, celebrities treat marriage like it's a subscription service. Some of them get remarried more often than they get their Pomeranian groomed. Honestly, marriage should come with an upgrade plan—like your phone. "Congratulations, you've completed two years without cheating! You're now eligible for a free spousal upgrade."

There is so much more to a successful marriage than the wisdom you are born with.

If you picked your spouse because you think you have great taste—well, you might. But if you picked them just on looks, be careful. I actually think really good-looking people have a lower chance of a successful marriage. It would be pretty difficult to get stats on this, but it just makes sense. They get asked out all the time, way more than the rest of us average folks. So basically, marrying a supermodel is like marrying a Baskin-Robbins—you may not be the only one sampling flavors. Good-looking people should have to do extra screening before marriage—like airport security, but for commitment issues.

Dating a 10 is like buying a Lamborghini—you think you're winning, until you realize you have to park it in public and pray nobody else takes it for a spin.

Jeff Bezos's new wife, Lauren Sánchez, clearly has excellent taste in men—her dating history proves she likes them rich, successful, and easy on the eyes. Her ex-husband, Patrick Whitesell, was a handsome, powerful Hollywood agent, married to her for 14 years. But apparently, that wasn't enough... because she decided to "upgrade" to Jeff Bezos. That's like trading in your sleek Ferrari for... well... the guy who delivers the Ferrari in a Prime box.

Her other famous relationship was with former NFL tight end Tony Gonzalez. Now that guy isn't just good-looking—he's so stunning that she went full-in and had a baby with him. And truthfully, who could blame her? Honestly, I'm sure plenty of women would line up for that honor. He's so handsome, even straight guys are probably like, "Yeah... I'd consider having his baby too." Okay, maybe that's a bit weird—but let's be honest: Tony Gonzalez is firmly in man-crush territory.

With Sanchez, one marriage with kids didn't last. A second relationship—with another child—also fell apart. So honestly, what are the odds that this marriage to Bezos is going to be the one that works?

How many people do you know who have been married 20, 30, 40 years, but are just managing to survive their relationship?

What is the biggest decision you are going to make in your life? Who you are going to marry, yet, when you spend more time figuring out the logistics of how to ship a Toy Story doll from Seattle to Miami, than figuring out how to actually keep a relationship passionate, you're in for a tough time. No wonder so many marriages crash—if your prep work for forever looks like Amazon logistics, don't be surprised when love ends up like a crushed box.

Just to be clear—I genuinely hope this marriage succeeds. I'm not rooting against Jeff and Lauren just so I can say, "I told you so." I chose a provocative title because I believe I can help change the trajectory of marriages—not just theirs. To get people to read my books, I need to hook them with an attention-grabbing subject. My hope is that once readers pick this up, they'll be inspired to explore my other books on dating and marriage, building self-esteem, and protecting their happiness from people who suck theirs dry.

I don't call myself a matchmaker—I'm a mate maker. I help people become the kind of person someone actually wants to marry. Unfortunately, I'm also unnervingly good at predicting which marriages will fail and which ones have a shot at lasting a lifetime. It can feel like a curse when you have that gut feeling that two engaged people you know are headed for a disastrous ending. Sometimes it takes decades to play out, but honestly, predicting a failed marriage isn't that hard—most of them are headed there anyway. You probably have better odds calling a doomed marriage than betting red or black at a roulette table.

The purpose of this book is twofold: to explain why this marriage might face challenges, and more importantly, to show you how to avoid those same pitfalls in your own relationships. I can make all the predictions I want, but if I don't give you actionable insight to prevent failure, this book would just be a waste of your time. I'm not trying to turn this into tabloid fodder—my goal is to teach you what it really takes to build a passionate, loving relationship with one person for the rest of your life.

John Gottman, the world-renowned marriage researcher, can predict with 94% accuracy whether a couple will divorce. The secret to a successful marriage isn't extravagant vacations, lavish gifts, or even three-day over-the-top weddings—it's the small, everyday actions and conversations that couples share that truly determine whether a marriage thrives.

He calls it "bidding for connection"—when one spouse reaches out, seeking engagement or a positive response from the other. In the early years of marriage, this comes naturally, but if you don't consciously register and reinforce these moments in your mind, you'll likely end up struggling—just like so many couples do.

Jeff Bezos is undeniably one of the greatest builders of an organization in history. He belongs in the business hall of fame with titans like Rockefeller, Carnegie, Disney, Jobs, Huang, Brin, Zuckerberg, and Musk—you name it. But marriage? That's a whole different hall of fame. And let's be honest, they don't teach "How Not to Blow Up Your Relationship" at Harvard Business School. You can ace supply chains, conquer cloud computing, and launch rockets into orbit… but try figuring out why your wife is mad without her telling you, and suddenly you're back in remedial math. The problem is, most people end up learning marriage the hard way—through trial, error, and plenty of bumps in the road. Yes, most marriages will have to go through the school of hard knocks. Unfortunately, it's those fake knockers that are a sign that you may have a tough marriage.

Let's start by looking at the issues in the Bezos–Sanchez marriage that are practically waving red flags right in front of us. After that, we'll dive into the skills you actually need if you want a passionate, lasting relationship with one person for the rest of your life. Because if this doesn't click, then I've failed—and trust me, I'm not about to list "marriage advice flop" on my résumé.

Grab some tea, buckle up, and let's do this—before Jeff's prenup lawyer beats us to the punch.

Coming soon...

www.ingramcontent.com/pod-product-compliance
Lightning Source LLC
Chambersburg PA
CBHW071828080526
44589CB00012B/946